Positive Intervention for Pupils who Struggle at School

Positive Intervention for Pupils who Struggle at School provides the resources and information primary teachers need to ensure a happy and effective school experience for all children, particularly those who are seriously struggling. This tried and tested intervention is designed specifically for those children who have been through all the standard interventions, to no avail.

Explaining the thinking behind the suggested modified curriculum, this innovative book considers the reasons why certain children experience difficulties and looks at how this curriculum addresses their needs and enables them to develop personal, social and emotional skills. The activities are chosen to develop and enhance skills for learning, including listening, speaking, concentrating, a positive disposition and a willingness to take on new challenges.

Helen Sonnet demonstrates how success has been achieved through this strategy and provides valuable information to help teachers to set up similar groups in their own schools, including how to:

- ensure firm foundations for the group
- select the children who will benefit most
- establish the structures and routine of a successful group
- assess the children's progress
- reintegrate children into their mainstream classes effectively.

In line with government initiatives this important and effective intervention strategy can make the world of difference, giving teachers new, proven strategies to enable them to support children who are struggling in mainstream primary schools.

Helen Sonnet is a lecturer, teacher and author with over thirty years experience of working with children with special needs. She currently works at Hayesdown First School in Frome, Somerset.

Positive Intervention for Pupils who Struggle at School

Creating a modified primary curriculum

Helen Sonnet

Routledge
Taylor & Francis Group

LONDON AND NEW YORK

First published 2010
by Routledge
2 Park Square, Milton Park, Abingdon, Oxon OX14 4RN

Simultaneously published in the USA and Canada
by Routledge
270 Madison Avenue, New York, NY 10016

Routledge is an imprint of the Taylor & Francis Group, an informa business

© 2010 Helen Sonnet

Typeset in Sabon by
Florence Production Ltd, Stoodleigh, Devon

Printed and bound in Great Britain by
The MPG Books Group

British Library Cataloguing in Publication Data
A catalogue record for this book is available from the British Library

Library of Congress Cataloging in Publication Data
Sonnet, Helen.
    Positive intervention for pupils who struggle at school: creating a modified
    primary curriculum/Helen Sonnet.
        p. cm.
    1. Education, Elementary – Curricula – Great Britain.   2. Remedial teaching –
    Great Britain.   3. School failure – Great Britain – Prevention.   4. Curriculum
    change – Great Britain.   I. Title.
    LB1564.G7S65 2010
    372.190941—dc22   2009025528

ISBN10: 0–415–55193–5 (pbk)
ISBN10: 0–203–86295–3 (ebk)

ISBN13: 978–0–415–55193–9 (pbk)
ISBN13: 978–0–203–86295–7 (ebk)

Contents

Acknowledgements

I would like to thank the staff of Hayesdown First School, in Frome, Somerset and in particular the head teacher, Liz Stokes, for their support and encouragement.

I am grateful to Simon Bishop, Nurture Group Coordinator at Christchurch School in Frome, for allowing me to use his parent questionnaire.

A special thanks to Clare Kennedy who has been my co-worker since the group's inception. She has been a real source of fun, creativity and encouragement.

I would also like to thank my partner, David Dayman-Johns, and my daughter, Katy Allcott, for their IT expertise in preparing this manuscript.

CHAPTER 1

Introduction

The current Primary Review has highlighted issues that teachers have been aware of and have been repeatedly raising for many years, namely 'that today's children are under intense and perhaps excessive pressure from the policy-driven demands of their schools . . .', and 'that the primary curriculum is too rigidly prescribed and, because of SATs, too narrow' (see www.primaryreview.org.uk).

In particular, vulnerable and needy children in our schools suffer from the Government's drive to raise academic standards with 'the aggravation of the gap between high and lower achievers . . .'. Children with special educational needs are more likely to be excluded, particularly during the primary school years. The Review notes that its findings suggest that 'teachers are finding it increasingly difficult to support children with special educational needs in mainstream primary schools'.

The Review concludes that '[t]here is a need to support schools as they strive to provide for children's needs rather than simply deliver a curriculum'.

Moreover, the Review considers the need for a reassessment of the aims of primary education, '[s]hifting from the currently narrow view of utility to one which is based on a more comprehensive and humane analysis of what is necessary for a productive adult life'.

My school, like countless others, was suffering from these issues relating to the National Curriculum. A small minority of the children were failing to learn satisfactorily. Moreover, none of the intervention strategies that had been introduced to help them were successful in the long term, which prompted me to look afresh at the purpose of these provisions to see where they were currently failing.

I concluded that, in spite of the good quality assistance in the classroom, the differentiation available and the extra-curricular support, many of the interventions were failing to address the root causes of the problems. I was convinced that these children could only really be helped by adopting a more radical approach that could not easily be delivered in their normal classroom setting. This would entail removing them from the classroom for a set period each day to follow an alternative curriculum that was better suited to their needs and offered a broader perspective.

At the same time, the children needed to experience an empathic, understanding attitude from the adults involved, such as is advocated for nurture groups. The perceived deficits in the children's skills make them vulnerable and uncertain, and they have a great need to be accepted and liked for who they are.

The alternative curriculum that we offered would be based on the aims and values deemed necessary to help these children towards enjoying both success in school and a productive adult life. In other words, we would be focusing on developing rounded individuals who possessed perceived competencies, a healthy view of self and a valued place in their world.

This book is intended, above all, as a practical resource for teachers who wish to set up a modified curriculum group in their school. I have not discussed in depth the various conditions that children may have, such as ADHD, Asperger's syndrome or dyslexia. Nor have I looked at strategies that deal with a particular focus, for example anger management. There are many excellent resources that deal with these issues, however, the focus of this book is to present a tried and tested alternative curriculum to help children who struggle.

There is a wealth of ideas available, but, especially with any new initiative, choosing the most effective interventions can be a minefield of trial and error. My school has had eight years to try out and test ideas, adopting those that are successful and discarding others that did not produce the desired outcomes. My aim in this book is to provide as comprehensive an action plan as possible. This, of course, does not mean that you have to follow the text to the letter. Rather, it should act as a guideline to help and support you as you embark on your own initiative.

The early part of the book examines the benefits of providing an alternative timetable and details what is involved. The book then considers which children would benefit from an intervention strategy of this type and gives examples in the form of case histories.

An example of a policy document on page 101 will help to focus your thoughts on exactly what you want to provide in your intervention. I strongly advise that you produce a policy document, as it will add status to your group. Moreover, it will demonstrate the level of forethought and care behind your intervention that can be useful, for example, during an Ofsted inspection.

PSHE plays a large part in our modified curriculum, as many of the children have emotional and behavioural issues, and a section of the book is devoted to how we make this a regular feature of our group.

We have found a themed approach to be very effective in the delivery of our curriculum and there is an example of how this can be put into practice on page 43, with many interesting and motivational activities.

I have also included the detailed plans for a twelve-week term of four afternoon sessions a week as an aid to help anyone starting up a similar group. These plans provide a suitable curriculum based on our experiences over the past eight years. At the beginning of each week, a prompt box reminds you of the resources you will need for each day's session, although you may need to read through the detailed plans to gain a full understanding of what is required. A sentence is included at the beginning of each day's plans that details the focus of the circle activities.

Finally, there is a section of photocopiable materials and other resources that can be adapted to suit the needs of your group.

CHAPTER 2

The benefits of a modified curriculum

The majority of children are able, to a greater or lesser degree, to access the National Curriculum. Their successful progress gives them the confidence and encouragement to continue to make an effort with their learning.

However, for the few children who do not succeed in their attempts to access the curriculum, their failure saps their confidence and breeds a fear that discourages them from further effort. They are also often aware that they do not make the same valuable contribution in their mainstream classes as other children and, therefore, feel unworthy and become demoralised. These children may then develop strategies, such as challenging or withdrawn behaviour, that enable them to avoid those situations they find difficult and reduce the incidence of continued failure.

As the children progress through the school and lack the inner resources to deal with frustration and other negative feelings, their behaviours become entrenched and often escalate, prompting the teaching staff to look for suitable intervention strategies. However, the strategies tend to treat the symptoms rather than the root cause of the problem and, therefore, have limited success. Adults within the school may come to see the children's behaviour as inherent character traits that cannot be changed, rather than a response to a difficult situation. However, with the correct intervention, these children can change. They do not have to be stuck with their problems and negative patterns of behaviour.

Within our school, providing a modified curriculum to a small group of children in a nurturing environment has been an extremely successful intervention. It has enabled all the children who have attended to return to their mainstream classroom and cope satisfactorily for the remainder of their time in the school. It has also eliminated the need for exclusions.

Providing a modified curriculum to a small group of children in this way has many benefits. Perhaps the most immediate benefit is the removal of the classroom pressures that generate fear of failure in these children, which, in turn, reduces the need for the avoidance behaviours that they have developed.

The small number of children in the group encourages a close-knit community that is an aid to learning. Moreover, with fewer children to look after, the adults have more time and opportunities to develop trusting relationships that enable the children to lower their defences.

One of the problems with the system in schools is the general assumption that children are, more or less, at a certain level of development when they enter Reception classes. However, this is often not the case. The alternative timetable and modified curriculum mean that the group can support the children's needs more effectively and take them forward from where they are at their actual current stage, rather than where they are expected to be.

So, for example, the timetable may include more activities with a PSHE focus to help develop the children's social skills and emotional learning. There is also a greater emphasis on communication and simple talking-based activities that give the children plenty of practice in developing language skills. Such development is a very important aspect of the children's learning because, if they do not understand the language of the classroom, they will not be able to respond appropriately and do what is required of them. Moreover, if their language is undeveloped and limited, they cannot communicate their problems effectively. Within the small group, there is greater opportunity for the children to practise understanding and following instruction, and to use expressive language.

Following instruction is a very important aspect of life in the mainstream class. Within the group, this can be practised as an exercise in its own right. Beginning with simple commands, the sets of instructions can become increasingly complex as the children learn how to focus on and retain the given information.

The greater flexibility in the delivery of sessions within the group allows for modification, depending on how things are going. This would be difficult to effect in a mainstream class. So, for example, children can be given longer to respond, activities can be curtailed or continued, and even omitted altogether, or extra activities can be added so as to meet the children's needs more effectively.

The children experience success very quickly and this encourages them to take on new challenges. They learn that, in spite of their problems, they can still achieve. Their success empowers them to have more control over their behaviour, as they see that they are able to change and improve. Some children are desperate to lose their 'naughty and disruptive' image, but their behaviour in the classroom has become entrenched and they do not know how to effect change. These children respond very quickly to the positive focus within the group and, almost from day one, may present a different persona, as they become aware that they are worthwhile and likeable and that they matter to someone in the school.

As the children's confidence grows, their avoidance behaviour diminishes. A positive change can often be seen by other adults within the school after a few weeks of the children joining the group.

The impact of this intervention strategy on the attitudes of the whole school cannot be stressed too highly. Members of staff no longer see naughty, disruptive and dislikeable children, but rather they see children with problems who can be helped to change if they are given the correct intervention.

When teachers hear the staff from the modified curriculum group talk about their difficult children in a more positive light, they begin to see another side to the children and can revise their own opinions. This approach also encourages members of staff to consider more fully the children's needs and where they may not be being met, and to develop a more empathetic approach. Empathy is a very important component of any approach, although it may not always be easy to see situations through the children's eyes. For example, it may be difficult to understand why a child finds assemblies very threatening and refuses to go into the hall. However, even though you may not always understand the threat, you can learn to accept that, from the child's perspective, it is very real to them and therefore not dismiss it so lightly. The impact, therefore, on the whole school is to generate a more hopeful attitude and a more caring ethos.

The modified curriculum incorporates routines and well-defined behaviour boundaries that create a secure environment. The approach of the adults is warm and relaxed in order to develop positive relationships and form close bonds with the children who attend. This is particularly important to create a more suitable learning environment for those anxious or unhappy children who crave emotional security. The familiar routines allow them to anticipate confidently what will happen.

Perhaps the greatest testament to the success of this intervention is the children themselves. They love being part of the group. Their attendance in school, alongside their behaviour, improves, as an upward spiral of success is created. They are able to return full-time to their mainstream classes, in due course, without further problems.

CHAPTER 3

Providing a positive identity

Providing a positive identity for children is paramount to their future success in the mainstream classroom. All the children who join the group have a history of failure. They arrive demoralised and disaffected, unable or unwilling to learn satisfactorily. They have no confidence in their ability to succeed in the classroom and, until the negative picture they hold of themselves is replaced with a more positive one, they will continue to fail. While giving children a more positive identity does not guarantee that they will achieve greater academic success, it will enable them to participate more fully in their mainstream classroom and cope with what is asked of them, in the knowledge that they too are worthwhile individuals.

The most important initial approach is to make the children feel welcome in the group, to show them that you are pleased to see them and that they are liked and valued. This is not always easy with some of the children who go out of their way to challenge authority or who have developed very annoying habits. This does not mean that poor behaviour is acceptable within the group. On the contrary, with such children it is important to be particularly stringent in your demand for appropriate and considerate behaviour. Any infringement of the group's rules (see page 10 for suggested rules) should result in an immediate consequence for the child, namely time away from the group to consider their actions. If the inappropriate behaviour is serious, one of the adults may need to talk to the child as well. However, once the consequence has taken place, the child can rejoin the group with a clean slate and immediately enjoy the esteem of the adults again. In this way, the children quickly learn that it is their behaviour, rather than themselves, that you do not like.

It is important that the children believe you like them. Their self-image is largely based on the reflected picture of themselves they receive from others. If the people they come into contact with react negatively towards them, these children will develop the opinion that they are not likeable and have little worth, and this will be reaffirmed with each negative encounter. It may be very difficult at times to respond with warmth and affection to challenging children, but if you consider how you feel when others are welcoming and pleased to see you, you will understand the impact that such a positive approach can have on them. Also, think of how you respond to people who are angry or cold towards you. You probably try to avoid their company wherever possible, but the children do not have the opportunity to remove themselves from a censorious adult's presence. It may take many weeks or months for your friendly approach to penetrate a child's self-protective shell, but, eventually, it will begin to have an impact.

Knowing that an adult in school likes them will allow children to believe that perhaps they have attractive traits after all. It can be a very liberating experience for children who generally elicit negative responses to feel the affection of and positive affirmation from an adult and figure of authority in their world.

Try to remember to make a point of welcoming each child with a smile and take time to listen to every individual's news and self-disclosures. You may find that some of the children come in to chat to you during their lunch break if you are setting up the room for an afternoon session. (Although this extra preparation means that you lose some of your lunchtime, having the room set up, with all the equipment and toys laid out and a circle of chairs ready for the children, is a very important factor in the smooth running of the group. These are not the sort of children who will sit quietly for ten to fifteen minutes while you organise the chairs and equipment.) Of course, a bonus of the children's lunchtime visits is that those who find it particularly difficult to cope in the playground are kept out of trouble.

A valuable strategy that is useful in helping to enhance the children's self-image is a positive focus on each child, such as a 'booster' display on the wall consisting of photographs of all the children alongside positive statements, either made by them or about them. For example, the children might complete sentence stems, such as 'I am good at _____' or 'I like to _____'. Other members of the group can be invited to complete affirming sentence stems, such as 'I like (name of child) because _____'. In an exercise such as this, it is a good idea to discuss positive attributes first to help the children think of appropriate endings, for example someone is kind, helpful, funny or a good friend.

During this daily circle time, you can frequently timetable activities that allow the children to express their personal views. For example, the children might complete sentence stems, such as 'If I was an animal I would be_____ because _____', 'If I was a firework, I would be _____ because _____', 'If I could have any Christmas present it would be _____' or 'My ideal holiday would be _____'. In this way, you are able to show the children that their views are valued and that every one of them makes an equal and important contribution to the group.

The second essential approach of the group is to ensure that the children experience success in what they do. We rarely ask the children to write during our sessions, as they can learn without having to record what they do. Also, for many children, asking them to write would simply repeat the pressures that they experience in the classroom, and that is what you are trying to avoid. With careful forethought, you can guarantee successful outcomes in art, cooking, science, gardening, drama, physical games and circle time activities.

Exploring a different theme each term, such as 'under the sea', 'the garden' or 'winter', enables you to produce a timetable of cross-curricular activities around the chosen theme. This is very useful, as, apart from having just one main focus for the children, they can build up very impressive displays of artwork to be admired by the rest of the school. The displays produced by our group are often used in the reception area so that all visitors and parents can see the excellent quality of the children's work. The praise they receive as a result of this further boosts their self-image.

Over time, the children begin to appreciate that they do possess skills and capabilities, can be competent and successful, and their achievements are applauded by their peers and other members of the school community.

As the children's confidence increases, they become more willing to take on new challenges. Within the group, they begin to develop more positive identities as children who are successful. It is interesting to note that, as this change takes place, the children will tackle and complete tasks in the group that are far more demanding than anything they would have attempted in the classroom. In their mainstream classes, they may perceive everything they are asked to do as too difficult but, conversely, within the group, they perceive everything they are asked to do as well within their capabilities.

However, in time, their new-found confidence will spill over into the classroom and they will begin to experience and build on success there as well.

Other factors within the group also help to boost the children's confidence and enhance their self-esteem.

Because the number attending is small (eight to twelve children), the adults can devote more time to each child than they might enjoy in their mainstream class. An adult can sit close to the children, encouraging their efforts and helping to keep them on track, offering assistance when it is needed.

In addition, the size of the group and the types of activities that we include help to foster positive group dynamics and boost positive interpersonal relationships. The children quickly take possession of the group and experience a great sense of belonging. They see themselves as special in terms of being part of our unique organisation. Parents report back to us how much the children love coming to the group and how being a member has changed their perception of school.

It is perhaps worth mentioning at this stage how the school community and the parents perceive our group, as this is an important factor contributing to its success.

All members of staff see the group as a valuable intervention strategy. However, this was not always the case and, in the beginning, several members of staff were sceptical about the value of such a group, or even downright hostile towards the idea.

Their objections generally fell into two camps. On the one hand, some teachers felt that we would be rewarding naughty children with a treat that they did not deserve. On the other hand, members of staff saw that two LSAs would be withdrawn from the general pool of help available in the afternoon, and they felt that this help could be put to better use. However, all the teaching staff has spent at least one afternoon in the group to see what happens there and to view their children in a different light. Also, after eight years of running, they have had sufficient time to witness the success of the intervention. Seeing the changes that have taken place in many of the school's most needy children has given the staff hope. Knowing that a successful intervention is available has removed the despair a teacher can feel of being 'stuck' with a difficult child.

Nowadays, the group is always talked about in glowing terms and the benefits that it brings to the children, and therefore the school as a whole, are recognised and valued. This attitude filters down to all the children in the school, who also see the group as worthwhile and important. We have not experienced any incidence of children being teased for attending or children not wanting to come because of any stigma that might be attached to their being part of our group.

The whole-hearted support of the staff is crucial for any group to develop a positive image within the school, as their attitude informs others of the valuable role the group plays within the school structure.

Occasionally, you may find that a parent is reluctant for their child to attend. This could be for a variety of reasons. They may have noticed that some disruptive children or 'slow learners' attend the group and see it as a 'dumping ground for bad children', and they don't want their child to pick up bad habits or undesirable language. However, if you talk to them about the whole range of needs that are catered for and how the tightly-structured timetable and rigid behaviour boundaries guard against inappropriate behaviour, they are usually reassured that this will not be the case.

They may be concerned that their child, who is already falling behind their peer group, will miss out on valuable 'learning' and fall even further behind. By explaining that their child is not accessing the National Curriculum successfully at the present time, you will be able to justify the need for an alternative approach. Attending the group is the most appropriate way of meeting the child's needs and helping them to develop better learning skills for the future through the carefully planned activities. The modified curriculum can devote more time to and place a greater focus on these skills at an appropriate level for the children than a mainstream class.

Some parents simply don't want their child to appear any different to their peer group. Once again, reassurance that the intervention is highly successful and will benefit their child in the long term is the most effective argument.

You can also reassure the parents that this intervention is a temporary measure and their child will rejoin their mainstream class on a full-time basis as soon as they are deemed able to cope successfully in that environment. To this end, they are assessed regularly to monitor their progress and see when reintegration is viable.

In any event, these and any other concerns that the parents might have are soon dispelled as they see the positive effects of the group on their child, especially when the improvements also become evident in the child's mainstream classroom. Moreover, the improved behaviour may be carried over to the home environment. This can be of great benefit to the whole family, where the child's inappropriate behaviour in the past has lead to the family being ostracised.

CHAPTER 4

Promoting positive behaviour

A further factor that greatly helps children to cope in school is the safety that the group offers in terms of its routines and behavioural boundaries. In so far as the former is concerned, the sessions can be carefully planned with this in mind, so that you can have the same activities in the same order and on the same day each week. A visual timetable is used to show the activities for each session, but the children quickly learn what they will be doing according to which day it is. This aspect is really important for those children who do not like changes to their routine, such as those with Asperger's syndrome.

As well as keeping to the same routines on a weekly basis, the greetings, circle activities and games that are included in a typical timetable are frequently repeated to ensure that the children are very familiar with them.

With a ratio of between eight and twelve children to two adults (sometimes we have three adults when an attending child is deemed to require one-to-one support), it is relatively easy to maintain rigid behavioural boundaries and help the children develop a sense of responsibility and ownership of their behaviour. We have four rules, namely:

- We play gently.
- We speak to people politely.
- We share the toys and equipment.
- We look after our equipment.

If you refer to these rules on a weekly basis, so that all the children are familiar with them, they know how they are expected to behave in the group. This is an ideal way to help children learn pro-social behaviour and, over time, the rules become internalised, so that the children are able to use them to regulate their own behaviour. It is also a good idea to remind them at intervals why these rules operate, asking them if they know the reasons for the rules. It is important that the children understand that the rules serve a purpose and are not simply arbitrary decisions by the adults.

Children can sometimes be helped to behave in an appropriate manner by having an adult sit close to them. The adult can prompt and praise the child and their close proximity can help the child relax, knowing the adult is in charge. In this way, the perceived stress that results in negative behaviour can be dispelled. Moreover, the adult can make positive choices for the child until the child has developed the coping strategies to make them for themselves.

Any infringement of the group's rules should result in an immediate consequence, such as asking the misbehaving child to sit on their own with a sand timer for one or two turns. During this time, you can ask them to think about their inappropriate behaviour and to come back to the group ready to behave as they know they should. Sometimes it is necessary to talk to a child if they are repeating actions and, occasionally, you might feel the need to show a child a cross face and voice in order to reinforce your message. Displays of anger by an adult should be quick and appropriate.

When children have temper tantrums, it is best to try and ignore them as far as possible and continue with whatever activity you are currently involved with. We have found this to be the most successful response.

However, if the child's behaviour becomes a danger to themselves or others, one of the adults should stand close by and request the child sits on a designated chair. The adult repeats the request until the child becomes calm enough to be compliant. At this stage, a turn of the sand timer is instigated.

Generally speaking, a child without an audience and not provoking the desired reaction soon forgets their anger. Children who have frequent outbursts of anger do not enjoy being out of control and rely on the adult to provide the discipline that they are unable to impose on themselves. We have found that repeating the same response in the same manner each time is the best way of dealing with these outbursts. Over time, as the child's needs are met and they learn more appropriate behaviour, the tantrums begin to diminish, until the child does not need to use them any more.

There are many useful strategies that you can use where anger is a particular issue of concern with a child. It can be helpful for a child to learn and understand that anger is a powerful feeling that we all experience. However, we have to find ways of containing angry feelings so that they don't become overwhelming and result in negative consequences for ourselves and others. Children can learn techniques to help dispel anger, such as counting slowly to ten, removing themselves from tricky situations, or square breathing (breathe in for a count of 6, hold for 6, breathe out for a count of 6, hold for 6, then repeat several times). As the children learn strategies for managing their anger, they feel happier that they have a means of regulating their behaviour and, thereby, avoiding unhappy consequences.

If children deliberately break or damage our equipment, there will be an appropriate consequence. For the next several days, they will not be allowed access to any toys and will instead play board, or similar, games with an adult. The message they need to learn is that they have to respect equipment that belongs to other people.

On the subject of respecting other people's equipment, there may be incidences of stealing within the group. Generally, this falls into two categories. Occasionally, children who are otherwise honest fall prey to temptation and take a toy or piece of equipment that they find exceptionally attractive. In these incidences, it is usually enough to explain why stealing is wrong and express disappointment and displeasure with their action.

However, there are also children who steal regularly and sometimes compulsively. The latter may take anything they can lay their hands on regardless of its apparent desirability. This is a more deep-seated and serious problem and could be associated with a variety of reasons.

A real understanding of ownership and stealing usually develops around the ages of between five and seven years. Before this age, children are very self-centred and impulsive and may take anything that they fancy. It could be that some of the children in your group have not reached this developmental stage yet.

Most parents begin teaching their children at a relatively early age that taking other people's property is wrong. However, if this has not happened with some of your children, or if stealing is carried out by other members of their family, they may not see the action as wrong.

Other children may steal for comfort because they feel unloved or are experiencing difficult situations at home or at school. They may have few toys at home or they may steal for attention.

Whatever the reason, punishment is not really a successful response. We have found the best way to deal with stealing is to talk to the children frequently about ownership of property. In simple terms, you can discuss how they would feel if someone took their new toy or their coat, for example. Ask them what would happen if everybody took home the toys and equipment that belonged to the group.

Where a child persists in taking things, you need to first ascertain that the child understands that this behaviour is wrong. You can then explain how you are going to try to help the child to be honest. Each day, the child will put their personal property into a tin. At the end of the day, they will receive this property back once you have checked their pockets and bags for other items that do not belong to them.

I remember one five-year-old girl who was very immature for her age and had a troubled home life. Her behaviour was generally impulse-driven and she was unable to cope with the routines of the classroom. She stole anything she could lay her hands on – other children's toys, their water bottles, scraps of paper, even my empty lunch box. She became very devious at concealing items, hiding them in her shoes, underwear, up her jumper and under her coat. This behaviour continued for a year or so, but, as she began to settle down and cope better with school life, she became happier and the stealing gradually stopped.

In addition to the consequences for poor behaviour, the children are given frequent recognition, praise and positive consequences for good behaviour.

Due to the nature and content of the timetable, that ensures the children are busily and suitably occupied, there is very little incidence of poor behaviour, and the minor squabbles that occasionally erupt between the children can usually be quickly dealt with. Even the quietest and most timid of children will feel safe in the group and soon begin to emerge from their shells.

A further way of helping to improve a child's self-image and promoting positive behaviour can develop as you get to know an individual. You will discover talents and aptitudes that have hitherto remained hidden. We found that one of our boys was exceptionally good at drawing stylised cartoon figures that were greatly admired by the other children and he became our artist-in-residence. He gained considerable kudos from drawing pictures for the other children to take home. One girl was good at organising the others at tidy-up time and another child knew all the specifications of most cars. A boy who could neither read or write was very talented at making things. He had his own workshop at home, and so had learned many woodworking skills and produced all kinds of useful items. The sad fact is that, while many of these skills could provide for a useful and productive adult life, they are not recognised and applauded within the current education system. The worry is that, with the narrow emphasis on academic learning, by the time these children reach adulthood, the mental health and behavioural problems that may have developed from their continued failure in school could prevent them from using these valuable skills in order to enhance both their own and other people's lives. Such aptitudes may not be recognised and applauded in mainstream classes, but in an intervention group there is the time and opportunity to allow the children to demonstrate their expertise and show that they can shine in some area.

Although the children are generally very happy to attend this kind of group, there may be occasions when they are reluctant to leave their classes. Rather than enter into a power struggle with a child in these circumstances, you could allow the teacher or teaching assistant to have a quiet word with the child and to bring them over when they are ready.

Occasionally, you may have a child who will decide, en route, that they are not going to the group. This behaviour often has more to do with gaining power than a genuine dislike of the intervention. Probably, the most successful way to deal with this problem is to give the child a 'powerful' role at the beginning of the afternoon session, such as taking charge of selecting who chooses the greeting each day or putting up the roster of helpers for each session. You will probably need to have a variety of 'special' jobs, so that when one loses its appeal you can have a substitute ready. In this way, you are also providing a positive position of power rather than the child using a negative one.

You can be flexible about children remaining with their classes for special events or outings if these are considered appropriate. However, because attending the group is the child's entitlement, they cannot be withheld as a punishment or to complete work.

CHAPTER 5

Developing social skills

As is to be expected, many of the children have poor social skills, so this is also a main area of focus in the modified curriculum. Having a small group of children means that you can give this subject more time than it would receive in the children's mainstream classes.

We include aspects of social skills development on a daily basis, discussing appropriate behaviour and responses to social situations. The children also have individual targets to work towards, as they are a valuable way of showing them what is desirable behaviour. The targets are reviewed and, if they have been reached, changed each term. They include:

- listening well when someone else is talking;
- sitting sensibly on my chair;
- speaking politely to others;
- helping to tidy up;
- remaining at the table until everyone has finished their drink and biscuits;
- sharing the toys and equipment.

The targets are displayed on laminated sheets containing a photograph of each child. Targets are written on to the sheets using a dry-wipe pen and the children can add a tick every day they are successful. When they have achieved ten ticks, they are given a smiley face to put on their sheets, the ticks are wiped off and the process begins again.

In addition to the learning skills already mentioned, many of the games and activities encourage the development of social skills and may have a positive focus on any of the following:

- recognising emotion in themselves and others;
- expressing feelings appropriately;
- taking turns;
- waiting patiently for a hesitant child to participate;
- learning from others;
- feeling confident to try something new;
- showing a positive disposition to participate;

- forming positive relationships;
- using agreed codes of behaviour;
- initiating activities with other children;
- working cooperatively within a group;
- abiding by shared rules;
- considering their own and others' needs.

One of the benefits of having a mixed-age group is that the younger children can learn appropriate behaviour from the older, more experienced children. Some of the children arriving in the Reception classes have come from homes where there are few behavioural boundaries and social skills are not recognised and taught. These children can use the older pupils as role models and soon follow their good example. In this way, they learn far quicker and with less verbal instruction from the adults. Moreover, being with older children for part of each day encourages more mature behaviour than if the children were with their own age peer group all of the time.

The presence of younger children has an equally beneficial effect on the older members. They become more caring and responsive to the needs of others and readily take on the responsibility of looking after and helping the younger members. This can be a huge bonus where the older child has significant problems engaging in positive relationships with their peers, as they are then able to demonstrate to others, and also appreciate themselves, their ability to get on well with other children and show friendship skills.

As well as individual targets, you could operate a different group incentive scheme each term. We try to incorporate an aspect of our current theme in these so, for example, if our theme was 'winter', we might have 'sensible snowmen', if our theme was 'space', we would use 'reliable rockets' or if our theme was 'under the sea' we would use 'friendly fish'. The items are each cut into twelve component parts and laminated. Although this may seem labour intensive at the time, after a few terms you can build up a bank of schemes that can be used over and over again.

You can decorate a display board with an appropriate background for each scheme and the children's names. When a child has behaved in the designated way, they are awarded a piece of their item alongside their name. When they have collected all twelve parts and achieved their finished item, they receive a reward. This might be choosing a game for all the group to play, being allowed to bring a friend from their class to an afternoon's session, being awarded a certificate in assembly by the head teacher or having their name and photograph on the 'superstars' board.

By running a whole group target scheme, you can frequently remind everyone that you will be looking out for children who are being sensible or friendly. The children enjoy watching their items grow and look forward, with great anticipation, to receiving their reward. Each time you award a child an additional part, remember to congratulate them for achieving the named target.

There are many opportunities during the sessions for pro-social skills to be taught and practised. For example, at refreshment time the servers are encouraged to politely ask each group member, 'Would you like a biscuit?' The children must reply in an appropriate way with 'Yes please' or 'No thank you', and then thank the server if they are given anything.

Playing games together is an ideal forum for learning valuable social skills. We frequently organise board games with the children where they practise taking turns, learning to play fairly and how to lose gracefully. The children are divided into two groups, each with an adult to supervise the activity.

Many of the group games, such as skittles, parachute games and team games also focus on these valuable attributes. Throughout the sessions, both adults consciously model pro-social behaviour and praise the children for their good efforts, so that this becomes a regular feature of group practice.

With a small group, there may also be opportunities to take the children into social situations outside of school. Obviously, outings need parental permission and the relevant procedures for risk assessment, but they can provide valuable real-life situations in which to practise important skills and appropriate behaviour.

For example, a visit to a local shop to buy the ingredients for cooking gives opportunities for the children to behave well in a public place and to communicate effectively.

Some children rarely, if ever, enjoy an occasion to eat out. A trip to a local café for a drink and cake or ice cream could be a huge treat for them. You may be able to take a bus journey to a venue or visit sites of interest with the children, which can be very important for any child who has previously been excluded from school visits due to poor behaviour.

As with behaviour in general, firm boundaries, adequate supervision and frequent practice will lead to appropriate behaviour on trips outside of school, especially when there is a treat in store for the children.

CHAPTER 6

Personal, social and emotional development

This is one of the most important subjects in the modified curriculum and is given a far greater focus than in the mainstream classroom. We use the social and emotional aspects of learning (SEAL) resources, small group booklets, as a basis for our programme but often adjust or adapt the sessions for the children.

It is easy to regularly include a focus on feelings and expressing emotions in an appropriate way during the circle time activities.

You can ask the children to show you appropriate 'faces' or to hold up the correct expression card for different situations (see page 117). Following on from this, you can ask them how they would feel and what they would do in the given situation.

Conversely, you may hold up an expression card and ask the children what might make them feel like this, for example, 'What might make you feel happy/sad/anxious/ excited?' A further activity involves placing the expression cards into a bag. The children take turns to pick a card out and think of a situation that would make them feel like their chosen card.

These activities can be repeated several times in a term without the children becoming bored of them.

You can investigate the language of emotions by playing games. For example, you could designate two areas in the room, one for happy words and the other for sad words. You call out different words and the children go to the designated area. They return to a central position after each turn. Some words to call are:

Jolly	Cheerful	Tearful
Miserable	Crying	Gloomy
Upset	Pleased	Joyful
Glad	Happy	Unhappy

A round of completing sentence stems can be a useful way of including a PSHE focus. For example:

'Something kind I did this week was _____ .'

'I was upset when _____ .'

'I get angry when _____ .'

You can use puppets to act out a short scenario with a moral message and then ask the children to comment. The puppets may quarrel and fall out, leading on to questions about how the puppets might feel in that situation and what they could do to make amends.

Cards that show a sequence of events are another useful tool. Sometimes the cards are set out in the correct sequence and the children are asked to interpret the situations and comment on the feelings of the characters shown. At other times you can display the cards randomly and ask the children to put them into the correct sequence, along with a commentary on the situations and events that are shown.

Reminding children of the group's rules and bringing their attention to their personal targets and the group incentive scheme is an everyday feature of good practice. This ensures that positive behaviour becomes commonplace within the group. It is interesting to note that, if a new and challenging child joins us, our well-established group is not influenced by their conduct. They ignore most inappropriate behaviour and carry on with the normal activities as though nothing was amiss. This is one reason why newcomers are quickly assimilated into the group. Not only do their actions attract very little attention, but they are also encouraged to join in and behave in a positive way by what they see and hear around them.

However, it is worth including a note of caution here. While one challenging child has little effect on the dynamics of the group, if two or more are introduced at the same time and largely occupy both of the adults' attentions, the rest of the group will begin to suffer from a lack of attention and trouble can start to creep in. It can be quite stressful at such times to maintain the balance of giving each child a positive focus and the more vulnerable members of the group may begin to revert back to former attention-seeking behaviours.

Moral messages can be further reinforced through a careful selection of reading material. For example, if the current incentive scheme has a focus on being kind, you can choose stories to read to the children that highlight this issue. You can then ask the children what features of the story were similar to the aims of the incentive scheme.

For some of the children, learning to manage their feelings and express them in an appropriate way is a very important lesson. One aspect of the adults' roles is to model positive behaviour as a demonstration for the children to learn from. The timetable and set-up of the group allows for inappropriate behaviour to be managed and discussed, rather than punished. Punishment has little lasting effect because it does not treat the root cause of the problem or teach the children a more positive way of behaving, so the offence is likely to be repeated in the future.

The beneficial effects of this approach can often be seen within weeks of children joining the group, with adults within the school reporting back a general improvement in a child's overall behaviour. Children become more polite and better mannered, less aggressive, more able to sit still and listen, more responsive to teaching and more disposed to join in activities.

As their confidence within the group increases, they are more willing to tackle new challenges and, eventually, this will be manifest in the classroom as well.

As stated previously, one of the aims of the modified curriculum is to create a more positive identity for the child that they are able to believe in. Once they begin to see themselves as capable and likeable, they will be less at odds with the world and the people around them. Having just one adult who likes, values and appreciates a child can have a very profound and positive effect on them.

CHAPTER 7

Enhancing the children's learning skills

The timetable is planned very carefully to realise the group's aims. As stated earlier, each session is divided up into small chunks of time so that no section lasts for more than thirty minutes. The activities are well paced to maintain the children's interest and deter inappropriate behaviour, although the children have between twenty and thirty minutes of free play in the middle of the afternoon.

The sessions always begin with circle activities. This part of the afternoon plays a very important role in enhancing the children's learning skills. There is a focus on looking, listening and thinking, as well as using expressive language.

As a long-time proponent of circle time, I believe that this seating arrangement has great benefits for the adults and children alike. It is easier for the adults to keep all the children focused and on track and to spot any inappropriate behaviour, while encouraging positive behaviour. The children are more likely to be engaged in the activities, as they see the others participate, and the shy, nervous child can watch and copy other children in the circle.

Each day, a different child chooses a greeting from a list of ten that are displayed. The child is selected by pulling a name out of a bag and the children enjoy the anticipation of who will be that day's lucky choice. This opener is important for grabbing the children's attention and empowering them to take control. It creates a positive group dynamic at the start of the afternoon that can be very important if any of the children have had distressing mornings in their mainstream classrooms or unfortunate incidents during the lunch break. The greeting each day provides a definitive line between the mainstream and modified curricula that these children follow, and they are encouraged to put their concerns behind them as they enter into the positive and relaxed atmosphere of the group.

The greeting is followed by two or three circle activities. Generally, one or two are language-based, while the other involves physical activity. The focus is on practising learning skills such as looking, listening, speaking and thinking. Children who could barely sit still for five minutes when they joined the group will be sitting in the circle and participating happily for twenty to thirty minutes within a couple of weeks. Incidentally, this is often one of the first improvements that become evident in their mainstream classroom: the children can sit and remain focused for longer periods.

Although numeracy is not actively taught in the group, number recognition and counting are regularly featured in the games. Every day, the members present in our group are counted so that we know how many to cater for at refreshment time.

We count round the circle together and then the child who chose that day's greeting counts on their own. Dice are used in some of our games and you can alternate between dice with digits and those with a shown quantity. Many of the circle activities involve counting or numbers in one form or another, without the pressure of being in a numeracy lesson.

We do, however, incorporate the pattern boards from Stern Structural Arithmetic (see useful resources) into some of the games, as many of the children have trouble establishing concrete numbers (quantity of physical items) with the abstract number symbols. So, for example, the children may be asked to take a number symbol from a box and match it with the correct pattern board or vice versa. If there are twelve children attending, they may be asked to get into groups of a given number by holding up the two, three, four or six pattern boards. Sometimes the children are put into two teams and asked to find either the odd- or even-numbered pattern boards, or the pattern boards are placed around the room and different numbers are called out for the children to run to.

Many of the children who join the group have trouble following instructions in their mainstream classes. You can help to improve this aspect of their learning by giving them tasks involving a set of instructions. Read each instruction twice or three times and pace your delivery according to the ability of your children. As the children improve, you can increase the number and complexity of instructions and speed up the delivery. Two examples are given below. You should decide what level is most suitable for your group. Give each child a piece of A4 paper and make sure each child has access to blue, red and green pencils or felt-tip pens. You may have to explain the terms 'landscape position' and 'portrait position', regarding the sheet of paper, if they are unfamiliar with these names.

Example 1

- Place your paper in the landscape position on the table in front of you.
- Write your name at the top of the page in the middle of the paper.
- If you have an 'N' in your name, write the letter 'N' under your name.
- Draw a red line down the middle of your paper from top to bottom.
- In the top right-hand corner, draw a blue box.
- In the bottom left-hand corner, draw a green circle.
- Write the first letter of your name in the blue box.
- Write your age in years in the green circle.
- Draw a blue wiggly line across the bottom of your page from left to right.
- Draw a smiley face anywhere on your sheet.

Example 2

- Draw a red circle in the middle of your page.
- Turn the circle into a face with two eyes, a nose and a mouth.
- Above the face, draw a blue wiggly line across your page.
- Underneath the face, draw a green square.
- In the middle of the square, write the number 1.

You can add drawing with rulers or around shapes if you think the children can manage such tasks.

You can also give the children instructions, one at a time, to perform manual tasks. For example:

- Collect the ball from the table by the door and give it to Jade.

- Put my book on the table by the middle window.

- Can you fetch me a red, blue and green pencil from the pot on the table.

- Can you build a tower that is six blocks high.

The language-based games involve the children speaking out in front of others and repeating forms and patterns of speech. The games are repeated on a regular basis so that the children quickly become familiar with what is required of them. It is important to include simple, response language games that do not require the children to think about what they have to say. The act of participating and speaking out in front of others is enough to begin with. Some examples of language-based activities are outlined below.

Button and key

One child (A) is asked to stand outside the circle wearing a blindfold. A second child (B) is given a button and key. The remaining children and adults say the following chant together:

'Down came (B's name), down came s/he, s/he is hiding the button and the key.'

While the above is being chanted, B walks around the circle and gives the button and key to two different players (C and D). Everyone then says:

'Who has the button?'

The person holding the button (C) disguises their voice and answers:

'I have the button.'

Child A has two guesses at C's identity. The question and answer are then repeated for the person holding the key (D). If A fails to guess a caller's identity, they can remove the blindfold and look.

This activity is fun and engaging, encouraging all the children to participate and speak out in front of others. The children need to learn a chant, follow rules, and watch, listen and concentrate on the action.

If a new child is very shy and will not yet speak out in front of others, you can say, 'It is someone very quiet' if they are holding one of the items. This usually prompts the correct guess.

My object

A selection of everyday objects, one for each child in the group, such as a toothbrush, a pen, a glue spreader, a watch and a spoon are placed in a bag. Each child in turn goes with one of the adults into a separate room or the corner of the room and takes an object out of the bag. The adult encourages the child to think of a simple clue describing their object. For a spoon the clue might be, 'You can use this to help you eat', for the glue spreader the clue might be, 'You can use this to help you stick things' and for the watch you could say, 'This helps you tell the time'. The clues need to be very basic in order for the describer to remember and repeat them and even then they may need whispered prompts.

Once the clue is agreed, the child returns to the circle to tell the other players. They put up their hands to show they have a guess and the child chooses someone to answer. This continues until a correct answer is given. Occasionally, you may have to give an additional clue if the object proves tricky to discover.

This activity is good for encouraging the children to look, listen, concentrate, speak out in front of others and use expressive language.

What am I?

For this activity, you will need a selection of pictures of familiar animals stuck on to card and laminated. Show the children the selection that you have before the game. It is important to do this as some children have undeveloped imaginations and without clues they simply cannot think of any animal. Other children might panic that they will not know the animal and are reassured by seeing what is involved.

Each child in turn has an animal attached to their back with sticky tape. They turn around slowly to show all the players their animal and then ask questions until they have discovered its identity. They might ask such questions as:

'How many legs have I got?'

'What colour am I?'

'Where do I live?'

'What do I eat?'

'Have I got a tail?'

If a child cannot guess correctly and runs out of ideas, they can ask for a clue from one of the players.

This activity is good for looking, listening, concentrating, speaking out in front of others and using expressive language. However, I do not think it is suitable for children from Reception and Year 1. I have found, to my cost, that this game can take forever with very young children as, for example, having been given the clues that they are big, grey and have four legs, they might ask 'Am I a fish?'

What could I take to _____?

Think of a venue to go to for a special activity. For example:

- for a picnic
- for a sleepover
- for a birthday party, or
- for the seaside.

Ask the children to put up their hands with ideas of items to take to the named venue.

In addition to language-based games, the children might complete a sentence stem in one round, for example:

'My favourite Christmas present was _____.'

'One thing I did in the holiday was _____.'

'My ideal holiday would be to go to _____.'

'My favourite dinner is _____.'

Some examples of active games are detailed below.

Afloat in a boat

The children and adults sit in a large circle. They pass a beanbag in a clockwise direction around the circle while saying the chant:

(Number in the circle, for example twelve) were afloat in a boat, there was a loud shout and one fell out.

The player who is holding the beanbag at the end of the chant must sit in the middle of the circle. They are given an opportunity to guess who will be out next time and, if they are correct, they rejoin the circle. The play resumes with an adjustment to the number in the 'boat'. Each time, the players in the centre are given the opportunity to guess who will be out next. The game continues until the circle is too small to make it viable.

■ This game is good for looking, listening, concentrating, speaking and counting.

Farmyard

The children choose three farm animals, such as a cow, a pig and a sheep. The players are then named 'cow', 'pig' and 'sheep' consecutively around the circle. The adult calls one or two categories and the players in the named categories swap seats. When the adult calls 'farmyard', everyone swaps seats. You can use variations of this game to fit in with any themes you might currently have. So, for example, if your theme was 'winter', you might have frost, snow and ice as your categories. If your theme was 'under the sea', you might have sharks, octopuses and shipwrecks.

■ This game is good for looking, listening and concentrating.

Rabbit's ears

Call the name of one child in the circle. This child puts their hands up on either side of their head with index fingers raised to represent half of a rabbit's ears. The children on either side put their index fingers up to the named child's fingers to complete the ears. The child calls out the name of another player who repeats the action, making up the ears with the children on either side of them. Children have to be very vigilant in this game and be ready to complete the ears of an adjacent 'rabbit'.

■ This game is good for looking, listening and concentrating.

Pass it along

The children pretend to pass objects around the circle from person to person, such as a furry kitten, a heavy object, a hot potato, a tiny crystal and a large box. Their mimes must reflect the object they are passing. Once the children are familiar with this game, they can choose the objects to be passed round.

■ This game is good for looking, listening, concentrating and using imagination.

A selection of source books for more circle activities is listed in the useful publications section at the end of this book (see page 106).

In addition to the circle games and activities, you can include other items to promote learning skills on a weekly basis. For example, on Tuesdays we play 'hunt the small toy' with a small, plastic dog. Two different children are chosen each week and take turns to hide the toy for the other to find. The remainder of the group helps the seeker by guiding them towards the hidden object with clues of 'cold', 'warmer', 'hotter' and 'scorching!'

On Thursdays we have the 'big picture contest' using a line drawing on A3 paper. We produce busy pictures of scenes, such as in a park, at the seaside or on a picnic. Each week, two small drawn details are added to the picture and the children must try and detect these. They score a point for each new addition they find and the adults score a point for any detail they fail to detect. With younger children you may need to have fewer items in the picture and make the additions quite noticeable, but you will know after a week or two whether your additions are too easy to spot, too difficult or just right.

Because the timetable adheres to its daily routine, the children look forward to these activities with anticipation on their allotted days.

Following on from the circle activities, there is a different main activity each day that provides a good opportunity to develop aspects of the children's learning.

For example, cooking involves the mathematical elements of weighing out ingredients, considering oven temperature and measuring baking times. And as far as language is concerned, the children learn cooking terms, for example 'creaming', how to describe the processes they engage in, and how to listen to and follow instructions.

Within their groups, they must take turns and have collective responsibility for the end product. The children enjoy the anticipation of eating what they have made and, on special occasions, for example when their parents visit, they have the opportunity to cook for other people and receive accolades for their efforts.

During art, the focus is on developing useful classroom skills such as cutting and colouring within lines, improving motor skills and manual dexterity through the use of different materials, gluing materials together precisely and developing creativity. This is a skill area in which children can show considerable improvement over a relatively short period of time. They can then demonstrate that improvement in the context of their mainstream class and thereby enjoy success in one area, at least, of classroom life. The more their confidence can be rebuilt in the classroom, the more new challenges they will be willing to take on.

Science activities focus on developing investigative skills, learning to use scientific language and working together cooperatively. Experiments are selected for their simplicity and quick results. For example, a fun way of demonstrating air pressure is to pierce a series of holes with a sewing needle around the circumference of a large, plastic bottle, about 7 cm from the base. The bottle is then filled with water to the brim and the lid tightly screwed on. When the lid is unscrewed, air pressure forces the water out through the holes. The children love to take turns to make the water flow out and this is something that they can repeat at home to amaze their parents with.

Another experiment the children love is to create their own 'volcanoes'. In pairs or small groups, they are given a yoghurt pot with a hole cut out of the base. The pot is inverted over a mound of bicarbonate of soda. If vinegar coloured with red food colouring is trickled through the hole on to the bicarbonate of soda, a chemical reaction causes an eruption of bubbling 'lava' to spill out of the 'volcano'. Once again, the experiment uses items that can be found in the home so the children can replicate this experiment outside of school.

The small number in the group and the intense daily focus on learning skills effects an improvement in the majority of children that is transferred to the classroom within a few weeks to two terms. The most obvious positive changes are the children's ability to sit still for longer periods, their increased concentration and a more willing disposition to participate in whole class activities.

CHAPTER 8

Selecting the children

In most classes there are one or two children who raise considerable concern by their lack of progress in the classroom. In addition to their lack of academic progress, they may show worrying behaviour traits, such as being withdrawn and difficult to reach or disruptive and challenging. These traits may have arisen because of the children's lack of learning skills and show their disaffection with the curriculum.

Most of the children who have been referred to us and attended the group have subsequently been able to rejoin their classes on a full-time basis successfully and there have been no exclusions from the school since the introduction of this intervention. A very few children have stayed with the group on a part-time basis, usually two sessions a week, giving them a valuable lifeline of support that enables them to cope for the remainder of the time in their mainstream class.

The children have come to the group with a wide variety of learning, developmental or social problems.

A few have been diagnosed as having Asperger's syndrome, developmental coordination disorder or ADHD.

Some have learning difficulties, such as a general global delay or dyslexia and others have social, emotional or behavioural difficulties resulting from life experiences such as neglect, abuse, the death of a close relative, the birth of a sibling or being adopted.

Whatever their problem, every child has benefited from their inclusion in the group and, in some cases, the positive changes have been startling and very quickly observed.

There is a set procedure to select the children who we think will most benefit from time in our group. When a place or places become vacant, the teachers are canvassed for any children they are particularly concerned about. The younger the children are who come to the group, the more successful the intervention, but problems are not necessarily obvious in children until Years 1 or 2 and sometimes older children join the school who are also in need of the intervention.

The teachers initially complete a Goodman's Strengths and Difficulties Questionnaire (see useful resources on page 106), a behavioural screening assessment. This covers twenty-five psychological attributes, looking at emotional symptoms, conduct problems, hyperactivity and inattention, peer relationships, and pro-social behaviour. If a child's score indicates an abnormal result, the class teacher then completes a Boxall Profile on that child (see useful resources on page 106).

The Boxall Profile, a set of diagnostic responses, was devised by Marjorie Boxall and colleagues to assess the emotional and behavioural needs of a child and is commonly used in nurture groups. It is made up of two sections, each containing thirty-four statements. The first section, called 'Developmental Strands', consists of statements that focus on a child's early personal and social development. These are displayed under the following headings:

Organisation of experience

- Gives purposeful attention
- Participates constructively
- Connects up experiences
- Shows insightful involvement
- Engages cognitively with peers

Internalisation of controls

- Is emotionally secure
- Is biddable and accepts constraints
- Accommodates to others
- Responds constructively to others
- Maintains internalised standards

The second section is the 'Diagnostic Profile'. The features in this section are displayed under the following headings:

Self-limiting features

- Disengaged
- Self-negating

Undeveloped behaviour

- Makes undifferentiated attachments
- Shows inconsequential behaviour
- Craves attachment, reassurance

Unsupported development

- Avoids/rejects attachment
- Has undeveloped/insecure sense of self
- Shows negativism towards self
- Shows negativism towards others
- Wants/grabs, disregarding others

The results of the children's Boxall Profiles can be displayed on histograms against the results of competently functioning children. This is extremely useful, as it shows the level of deviation of each child's behaviour from the norm and the specific areas that are most affected. The results can, therefore, be used in planning strategies and targets for the children. Moreover, it is often the case that, through administering the Boxall Profile, the children's teachers gain a greater insight into and understanding of their behaviour, thereby helping them to deal with the children more sympathetically.

The additional value of the Boxall Profile is that it can be administered at regular intervals (we use it twice yearly, in June and November) to show where progress is being made and the results will indicate, alongside their teacher's evaluation, when a child is ready to begin the process of reintegration to being with their class full-time.

In general, the children remain with the group for between two terms and two years, depending on their progress.

Some children start school with little formal training. At home, they have few routines and even fewer behaviour boundaries. They are consequently confused and upset by the strictures of the school day. They respond to the difficult situation with challenging behaviour and may be very disruptive, as the adults encourage them to conform.

We have such a child currently in the group. He lives with a single mother, who also has learning difficulties, and who is unable to cope with the child's behaviour. He is not toilet trained yet and is unable to communicate effectively. When he joined the group, he would not sit in the circle for more than a few minutes. His behaviour was impulse-driven, often bizarre, and he would kick and bite any adult who tried to thwart him. However, after half a term, with patient encouragement, rewards (he likes to tick his target sheet) and because the daily routine never alters, he has learned how to sit in the circle for the required amount of time. He joins in the activities to the best of his ability and has made real progress.

Such children greatly benefit from a period in the group, where the routines, emphasis on learning skills and rigid behaviour boundaries in a tightly structured timetable inform the children very quickly how they should behave. Teachers often see a marked improvement within a matter of weeks as the children learn what is expected of them in school. Moreover, because of the positive affirmation within the group and an emphasis on achieving targets and earning desirable rewards, the children see the benefits of complicit behaviour. These children may be ready to reintegrate back to full-time classes within two terms.

Other children have already developed entrenched negative behaviour patterns towards their primary caregivers by the time they enter school. If they experience a similar attitude from their teachers, they will continue to reciprocate with their learned responses. These children particularly need the therapeutic approach, over time, that the group can offer if they are to change and, even with such care and consideration, it can be a long, slow process.

Children with Asperger's syndrome and ADHD benefit from the highly-structured sessions. They feel safe in an environment that offers them routines and guidance on how they should behave. In the sometimes confusing and changing world of their mainstream classroom, they can become difficult, disruptive and even violent. The group can offer such children a lifeline of stability that can make the difference between their remaining in school and being excluded. Sometimes, children with Asperger's syndrome remain with the group for at least two afternoons a week for most of their school life, as they need the safe base that it can offer them.

Children with general global delay or of low academic ability really flourish when they join the group. Because the modified curriculum offers a broader perspective than the National Curriculum and is not driven by academic targets, the children experience different criteria for success. In fact, guaranteeing success is a focus of the approach to enhance their self-esteem and help the children towards a more positive identity.

These children can be deeply unhappy at school, where they face failure on a regular basis. As the gap between their capabilities and those of their peers widens, they become aware of their lack of success and how they may be viewed in a negative way by their classmates and even some adults. These children may have become so disheartened and disaffected that they have switched off from the learning process and display avoidance behaviours in class.

The group guarantees individual success for all the children and there is a daily focus on basic learning skills that they need to help them to cope in their mainstream classes.

Once again, an overall improvement in behaviour and attitude to school can be seen very quickly in these children. The boost to their self-esteem and confidence, and the knowledge that they do possess skills and competencies, encourages them to participate more actively in the classroom. Any knocks that they may receive are not as damaging as previously, because they can be counteracted by success during the afternoon sessions. Being part of a group such as this can have a tremendous impact on children's perspective of school. Many of the children have gone from hating school and with a poor record of attendance to being happy and at school for the majority of the time. Sometimes, children who seem immature for their age catch up with their peer group and experience no further problems. A few of the children with very low academic ability have remained with the group on a part-time basis, usually two afternoons a week, for most of their school life, so that they can satisfactorily cope with the academic pressures of the curriculum in their mainstream classroom.

The quiet, withdrawn children experience a similar, albeit slower level of success. When they first join the group, we are very careful not to put any pressure on them to participate in the activities. As explained previously, the routines that are in operation offer security. Moreover, the circle activities that form a regular part of the timetable are repeated frequently so that the children feel safe with their familiarity. The circle activities are also chosen because they are fun and engaging and, as they are conducted in a circle, all the children can see what to do by watching the other participants.

Gradually, the quiet children are encouraged to join in, often in whispers to start with. By the time they have been with the group for a few terms, they are participating as actively as the other children and, as their confidence grows, they begin to speak out in class as well. These children may stay with the group for up to two years before they are confident enough to remain with their classes on a full-time basis.

For children with development coordination disorder (dyspraxia), who find it difficult to concentrate on the work in their mainstream class, the modified curriculum and small group setting offer ideal training to develop their ability to be actively attentive. With fewer sensory demands that distract and disrupt these children's ability to concentrate, they are able to make progress within the group. Moreover, the structure and pace of each session that involves changes of activity help to keep the children alert.

Children with emotional and behavioural difficulties are usually the most difficult to help and in these cases it is the slow drip, drip of persistence that eventually pays off. They may not be interested in achieving success in what they do, have little regard for positive affirmation and be well entrenched in negative behaviour patterns. These children need different motivational forces and we have found that the most successful approach is to show them that they are liked and valued, however hard this can be at times for us. We retain very strict behaviour boundaries with them, continue to praise their positive behaviour and try to employ them in responsible positions within the group.

Quite often, these children will slowly develop a positive attachment to one of the adults and this will generate a desire to please in the child. This can be used to promote more positive behaviour and begin an upward spiral of success. However, it may take two or more years to achieve a real and noticeable improvement in these children.

The overall make-up of the group needs consideration in relation to gender and behaviour problems.

Although the ideal would be to have a fifty-fifty mix of boys and girls, 80 per cent of special educational needs (SEN) children are boys and this has always been reflected in our group. The number of girls has varied from two to four, but never more than this. It is easier to create a balanced mix of those children who act out and those showing withdrawn behaviour, which is vital for the success of the group. Moreover, some of the most challenging children have one-to-one support. This essential help should carry on within the group, so that you can continue to accommodate all the most needy children.

CHAPTER 9

Case studies

Ellie

Ellie was a Year 3 child when she joined the group. She was big for her age, loud, disruptive and, at times, aggressive. She had very low academic ability and was still unable to read or recognise numbers. Her behaviour, both in class and around the school, generally was met with exasperation by other children and adults alike.

We decided that it was very important to show Ellie that she was likeable and possessed skills. The first of these could be extremely difficult at times as Ellie was the sort of child who could never resist touching things that she should not. Moreover, she was like a bull in a china shop and acted before considering the consequences of her actions. However, instead of becoming irritated, we treated her misdemeanours with humour and tolerance and, most importantly, we always showed her how pleased we were to see her. At the same time we worked on her social skills, reminding her daily of good manners and considerate behaviour towards others.

In class, Ellie put the minimum amount of effort into her work. The only objective was to complete a task as quickly as possible. Gradually, over the following weeks, Ellie experienced considerable success in the activities that we did. She baked superb cakes, she created attractive artwork and took the lead roles in our drama productions. Moreover, as one of the older children in the group, she adopted a motherly role to the younger children and was brilliant at organising the clearing up and putting away of equipment and toys.

Being liked, being praised and feeling that she was good at something in school had a tremendous effect on Ellie's overall effort and behaviour. For example, when she first joined the group, her colouring-in was at the level expected of a Reception child. However, within weeks she was producing beautifully and painstakingly coloured pictures. The dinner ladies commended her teacher on her good manners at lunchtime and the teacher, herself, found Ellie less disruptive in class.

The consequence of Ellie's improvement was that the staff and other children started to like her more and, even when she left the group, her passage through the school was easier and happier than before.

Harry

Harry, a Year 2 child, was diagnosed with Asperger's syndrome. He was very difficult in class, called out constantly, refused to work with other children and could be aggressive if thwarted. He had his own little space in the classroom, where he could be alone and he also had occasional one-to-one support, but nevertheless he was still very disruptive. When he came to the group, his teacher was very glad of the respite so that she could concentrate fully on the other twenty-nine children in her class.

As is often the case, humour played a large part in effecting an improvement in Harry, plus a never-ending interest in the specifications of washing machines and discussions about the best models. (When Harry went missing on family holidays, his parents always knew they would find him in the laundrette.) We reminded him constantly, calmly and without anger of the need to remain quiet when someone else was talking. We enforced very strict behaviour boundaries with him and he was often asked to sit alone and consider his actions. In addition, we frequently used circle time to examine emotions and feelings in ourselves and others, and we encouraged him to join in the group activities.

By the time Harry went into Year 3, he was more or less a fully integrated member of the class. He still called out on occasion, but in general he was biddable and well-motivated. He remained with the group on a part-time basis until the last term of Year 4.

Alex

Alex joined the school in Year 2. He was adopted and had considerable learning difficulties. He was very withdrawn and quiet and would not join in any activities.

We never put pressure on Alex to participate, but in the circle activities he could watch what every other child did and gradually learned what to do. If a response was required, we might make suggestions for him to nod agreement or disagreement or the other children could offer suggestions for Alex to choose from. In one particular game (button and key, see page 21), a child wears a blindfold and a second child gives two objects to members of the circle to hold. We then ask who is holding each object and those two children respond, disguising their voices. The child wearing the blindfold has to guess the identity of either child. If Alex was holding an object and would not respond, I would say, 'It's someone very quiet' and his identity would invariably be correctly guessed. None of the children commented on this procedure and it avoided unwelcome pressure to respond being placed on Alex.

Because many of the circle games are so engaging, once he was familiar with the activity, Alex would respond automatically before he had time to become self-conscious. By the time he was in Year 4 and a senior member of the group, Alex's hand was always the first to be raised. He joined in everything with confidence and assuredness. He also participated well in class and was not discouraged when his contributions were incorrect.

Joe

Joe was a Year 4 pupil when he came to us, during our first year. Had the group already been in operation, he would certainly have joined us earlier. He was the saddest child I have ever seen. He came from a background of neglect, in a single parent family where his mother was affected by alcohol and drugs. He was thin, listless and showed little interest or enjoyment in anything he did at school, although academically, he was quite bright.

To begin with, he did not want to join in any of the activities and needed to be cajoled to take part. He was, by and large, unresponsive to our friendly overtures, preferring to sit alone and morose.

However, as the year progressed, he slowly began to thaw. One of our greatest joys in the group was to witness this boy smile for the first time. By the end of the year, we discovered that he had a sharp, intelligent wit. He looked forward to joining the afternoon sessions, happily participated in all the activities and became quite chatty and communicative.

He was also more involved in his mainstream lessons and working at the level that his ability indicated he should be achieving.

Jake

Jake came to us as a Year 3 pupil and developed into a real 'Jekyll and Hyde' character. At the time that he joined the group, he was driving his class teacher to despair. He had considerable learning difficulties and reacted to his lack of success with escalating poor behaviour. When the class were enjoying carpet time, Jake would call out facetious remarks or make distracting noises. When he was set to work with a helper, he would refuse to cooperate. This had become something of an established routine, with the teacher becoming more and more exasperated with him.

As soon as Jake joined the group, we treated him as someone who could be sensible, responsive and well behaved. We made a particular effort to show Jake that we liked him and were pleased that he was a member of the group. Coupled with the more suitable curriculum that allowed him to function at a level within his capabilities, without this being noticeably remedial, our approach had an immediate effect.

When I collected Jake from his classroom, I might find him standing outside the door or rolling around on the classroom floor, but on the walk over to our premises he underwent a transformation, becoming sensible and compliant. These roles would be reversed if I had to take Jake back to his classroom for any reason. The pleasant, likeable boy would start to make silly noises and become difficult to manage on the walk back.

Jake was convinced that it was the behaviour of the members of staff rather than his own behaviour that made the difference.

It took a long time for the positive attitude to transfer back to the classroom but, after two terms with us, Jake's confidence had increased sufficiently to allow him to tackle reading in a more meaningful way. As his reading improved, so did his behaviour, but it took a change of teacher to really establish a more positive pattern of behaviour in him.

Examples of the results of the Boxall Profiles

As explained previously, we use the Boxall Profile both to demonstrate suitability for joining the group and, thereafter, to assess progress.

The first examples are from a Year 2 boy taken in November 2006 and again in June 2007. The original profile shows a child with poor concentration and listening skills. He is insecure, lacks independence and needs constant support to finish tasks. He shows low self-esteem, finding it difficult to express his own needs and consider the needs of others. This is a child who is not comfortable in social situations and cannot work successfully within a group.

He also has a problem making attachments, has a profound lack of trust in others and is without interest or motivation. He is very sensitive about his own worth and overly worried about making mistakes in his work, so achieves very little. He cries every morning and clings to his mother when she tries to say goodbye to him.

The profile of 2007 shows a child who is functioning at a level much closer to the norm. In spite of a small increase in his score for negativism towards self, the child is now considerably more settled in his mainstream class. He is happier, more confident, working well and making good progress. He is able to interact successfully with his peers and has developed some good friendships.

It was thought wise to keep the boy in the group on a part-time basis during the transition from Key Stage 1 to Key Stage 2, but he was fully integrated back into his mainstream class by October 2007 and has had no further problems.

The second set of examples is from a girl in Year 2. Her original profile, taken in July 2004 (at the end of Year 1), shows a child who lacks independence, has poor concentration and finds it difficult to sit still. She is unable to express her needs in an appropriate manner and cannot share or interact successfully with others. She shows a fragile self-image, fears rejection and is unusually sensitive to criticism, at the same time being difficult to reach or motivate. She shows negativism towards herself and others, lacking trust in other people. Her behaviour is impulse-driven and she is unable to reflect on her actions. This girl is very difficult to handle in class and has frequent emotional outbursts. She is generally uncooperative with the adults and often angry and aggressive with her peers. Her behaviour is so extreme that she failed to achieve any score in some of the developmental strands.

Her final profile taken in January 2006 shows the huge improvement in this girl. Her behaviour is at a level commensurate with her peer group and her chart shows near normal levels of behaviour, although she is still in need of some reassurance. By the time this girl was in Year 4, she was no longer seen as a pupil who had special needs.

Year 2 boy

Developmental strands

Organisation of experience

	Competently functioning children	Year 2 boy October 2006	Year 2 boy June 2007	Difference
Gives purposeful attention	18–20	13	17	+4
Participates constructively	10–12	4	10	+6
Connects up experiences	7–12	3	8	+5
Shows insightful involvement	14–20	5	16	+11
Engages cognitively with peers	7–8	4	6	+2

Internalisation of controls

Is emotionally secure	11–12	4	9	+5
Is biddable and accepts constraints	14–16	11	12	+1
Accommodates to others	19–20	6	17	+11
Responds constructively to others	7–8	2	6	+4
Maintains internalised standards	6–8	5	7	+2

Diagnostic profile

Self-limiting features

Disengaged	0–1	11	2	–9
Self-negating	0–1	12	3	–9

Undeveloped behaviour

Makes undifferentiated attachments	0–1	0	0	0
Shows inconsequential behaviour	0–1	1	0	–1
Craves attachment, reassurance	0–0.5	0	0	0

Unsupported development

Avoids/rejects attachment	0–0.5	14	3	–11
Has undeveloped sense of self	0–1	4	0	–4
Shows negativism towards self	0–1	0	2	+2
Shows negativism towards others	0–1	4	1	–3
Wants/grabs, disregarding others	0–1	0	0	0

Year 2 boy

Developmental strands

Charts show child's scores as a percentage of score obtained by competently functioning child.

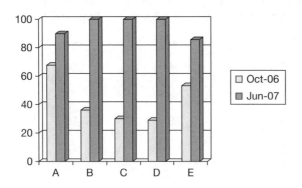

A Gives purposeful attention
B Participates constructively
C Connects up experiences
D Shows insightful involvement
E Engages cognitively with peers

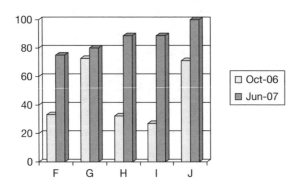

F Is emotionally secure
G Is biddable and accepts constraints
H Accommodates to others
I Responds constructively to others
J Maintains internalised standards

Year 2 girl

Developmental strands

Organisation of experience

	Competently functioning children	Year 2 girl July 2004	Year 2 girl January 2006	Difference
Gives purposeful attention	18–20	4	20	+16
Participates constructively	9–12	0	12	+12
Connects up experiences	7–12	2	12	+10
Shows insightful involvement	14–20	0	16	+16
Engages cognitively with peers	7–8	0	8	+8

Internalisation of controls

	Competently functioning children	Year 2 girl July 2004	Year 2 girl January 2006	Difference
Is emotionally secure	11–12	1	12	+11
Is biddable and accepts constraints	14–16	0	15	+15
Accommodates to others	19–20	0	16	+16
Responds constructively to others	7–8	1	6	+5
Maintains internalised standards	6–8	0	8	+8

Diagnostic profile

Self-limiting features

Disengaged	0–1	10	0	−10
Self-negating	0–2	0	0	0

Undeveloped behaviour

Makes undifferentiated attachments	0–1	12	0	−12
Shows inconsequential behaviour	0–1	12	0	−12
Craves attachment, reassurance	0–0.5	12	6	−6

Unsupported development

Avoids/rejects attachment	0–0.5	12	0	−12
Has undeveloped sense of self	0–1	12	2	−10
Shows negativism towards self	0–1	9	0	−9
Shows negativism towards others	0–1	3	0	−3
Wants/grabs, disregarding others	0–1	8	0	−8

Year 2 girl

Developmental strands

Charts show child's scores as a percentage of score obtained by competently functioning child.

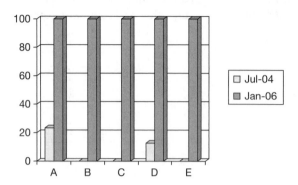

A Gives purposeful attention
B Participates constructively
C Connects up experiences
D Shows insightful involvement
E Engages cognitively with peers

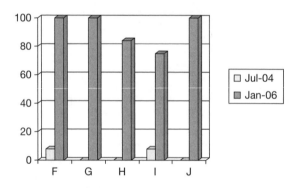

F Is emotionally secure
G Is biddable and accepts restraints
H Accommodates to others
I Responds constructively to others
J Maintains internalised standards

Examples of attendance figures

The following examples chart the school attendance figures of two children who joined our group. The improvement shown is typical where poor attendance is an issue.

- Child A started attending the group in October 2004. By the end of 2006, his attendance had risen from 77 per cent to over 93 per cent. This was a huge improvement and a further factor that contributed to his improved performance in school.

- Child B started in February 2005 and, although the improved attendance figures are still not as good as they should be, they nevertheless show a marked rise from 69 per cent to 87 per cent.

I believe that, as the children became happier in school as a result of attending the group, they were less inclined to proffer excuses to stay away from school. It was interesting to note that, if the children were absent, it was more likely to be a day when they did not attend the group.

At the same time, their improved behaviour and performance in class resulted in fewer worrying and negative reports to their carers, thus encouraging them to pursue a more active policy of ensuring their child came to school.

Furthermore, improvements in school were often reflected at home, resulting in better relationships between the child and their primary carer.

Case studies

Child A: Attendance summary

**Summary: 1 September 2003 to 23 July 2004
(am to pm)**

	Sessions	%
Attendances	268	78.6
Authorised absences	34	10.0
Unauthorised absences	39	11.4
Possible attendances	341	
Including		
Approved educational activity	0	0.0
Lates before register closed	7	2.1
Lates after register closed	3	0.9
Unexplained absences	0	0.0

**Summary: 1 September 2004 to 22 July 2005
(am to pm)**

	Sessions	%
Attendances	293	77.1
Authorised absences	49	12.9
Unauthorised absences	38	10.0
Possible attendances	380	
Including		
Approved educational activity	0	0.0
Lates before register closed	10	2.6
Lates after register closed	16	4.2
Unexplained absences	0	0.0

**Summary: 5 September 2005 to 25 July 2006
(am to pm)**

	Sessions	%
Attendances	353	93.4
Authorised absences	6	1.6
Unauthorised absences	19	5.0
Possible attendances	378	
Including		
Approved educational activity	0	0.0
Lates before register closed	0	0.0
Lates after register closed	1	0.3
Unexplained absences	0	0.0

Child B: Attendance summary

**Summary: 1 September 2003 to 23 July 2004
(am to pm)**

	Sessions	%
Attendances	237	69.5
Authorised absences	50	14.7
Unauthorised absences	54	15.8
Possible attendances	341	
Including		
Approved educational activity	0	0.0
Lates before register closed	2	0.6
Lates after register closed	0	0.0
Unexplained absences	0	0.0

**Summary: 1 September 2004 to 22 July 2005
(am to pm)**

	Sessions	%
Attendances	332	87.4
Authorised absences	12	3.2
Unauthorised absences	32	8.4
Possible attendances	380	
Including		
Approved educational activity	0	0.0
Lates before register closed	0	0.0
Lates after register closed	0	0.0
Unexplained absences	0	0.0

**Summary: 5 September 2005 to 25 July 2006
(am to pm)**

	Sessions	%
Attendances	331	87.6
Authorised absences	27	7.1
Unauthorised absences	20	5.3
Possible attendances	378	
Including		
Approved educational activity	0	0.0
Lates before register closed	1	0.3
Lates after register closed	0	0.0
Unexplained absences	0	0.0

CHAPTER 10

An alternative curriculum

It is very important, before setting up any intervention strategy, to have clear aims and goals. These are essential to inform the work that you do, as, without clear guidelines, you are liable to stumble along, trying everything that appears to be successful and achieving little in the long term.

The greatest benefit in modifying the curriculum is that it is not driven by academic targets. Rather, the direction is determined by what you hope to achieve.

In our group, I considered the following aims essential for a successful outcome to our intervention:

- creating a more positive identity for the children;

- enhancing the children's learning skills;

- enhancing the children's social skills.

If these aims could be achieved, I felt sure that the children would be better able to cope with the demands of their mainstream classroom.

After some deliberation, the school management team considered that a full-time intervention group would not be possible or appropriate for our school. This was based partly on allocation of funding within the school, and also on the experience of other schools. To remove a child full-time from their mainstream classes can create problems with reintegration. However, there is also a need to ensure that their time allocation with the group is sufficient to provide real and lasting benefit for the children.

You may find, as we did when we looked at their timetables, that most of your children have considerable support in either small groups of four or five, or even one-to-one, during numeracy and literacy. Mornings also tend to offer more structure, better suited to keeping the children on-track.

Their inability to function successfully in their classrooms may become more noticeable by the afternoons, when, not only are they becoming wearied by the demands of the curriculum, but also they may be unable to cope with the more relaxed structure and less available assistance. Of the five afternoons available in our school, we decided that the children would stay with their classes on a Friday afternoon so that they could enjoy Golden Time together. If you are unfamiliar with this concept, it is a period when the whole class enjoys choosing time to celebrate keeping the Golden Rules, and was devised by Jenny Mosley as part of her Quality Circle Time initiative. The remaining four afternoons, they would come together in a different setting and follow the timetable that had been devised for them.

We have found that this level of intervention is certainly sufficient to effect positive changes in the children.

With help from the school's management team, a policy document was written stating our aims and the provision we would offer (see page 101). It is worthwhile taking time to devise the most suitable timetable to achieve your aims. You need to provide a curriculum that ensures the children are fully engaged, but at the same time they need to be freed from the pressures of the mainstream classroom.

An ideal timetable is to split sessions into twenty to thirty minute slots. A well-paced afternoon with several changes of activity will help to maintain the children's interest, and allow less time for them to wander off track and engage in unwelcome pursuits.

- The first part of the afternoon, when the children are freshest, is best utilised for circle work, during which time you can focus on developing learning and language skills and promoting positive group dynamics.

- A main activity, such as art, cooking, science, drama or gardening can follow, after which the children enjoy a period of free play, mid-afternoon.

- At the end of the free play session, the children come together for a drink and biscuit, and the afternoon ends with a story and singing/clapping rhymes.

We have found this timetable to work very well, with a few minor adjustments from time to time. For example, there have been occasions when the children engaged in imaginative play that became too boisterous. If such a game becomes a 'craze' that the children repeat, it helps to increase the time spent on circle activities and, temporarily, structure the free play session, for example with jigsaw puzzles or board games. A few days of such intervention usually guarantees a return to more suitable play.

The afternoons fly past and the children, for the most part, are happily occupied and engaged. Being busy is good training for their eventual reintegration to their mainstream classes.

CHAPTER 11

Using a themed approach

Using a different, themed approach each term can be of benefit in creating a focus that lasts for a considerable time. The diversity of subjects and themes in the mainstream classroom can be confusing for the child with learning difficulties. Insufficient time may be spent on any one area before moving on, for some children, with the result that they never fully grasp a concept that is being taught.

Using a cross-curricular approach within a theme allows for greater familiarity as you can remain with each focus for the entire term and are able to revisit areas to reinforce learning.

To give an example of this approach, there are details of the work from one of the themes below.

In the garden

Incentive scheme

A large sunflower is prepared for each child consisting of a centre, on which their name is written, nine petals, a stem and two leaves (see photocopiable resources, page 121). The flower centres are displayed on a suitable 'garden' background and the children collect the remaining twelve parts to complete their flowers. You can put up a suitable title to your incentive scheme, depending on what your current focus is, for example, 'our good manners garden', 'friendly flowers' or 'sensible sunflowers'.

Ensure that you have a worthwhile reward for each child as they complete their flower, such as choosing a game for the group or bringing a friend from class to one of the sessions.

Circle activities

- Many of the circle games and activities that are used can be modified to accommodate the current theme. For example, in the game **Farmyard**, where children are usually named 'cow', 'pig' and 'sheep' consecutively around the circle, you can ask them for three things that might be found in a garden instead and use those names. Each time you call one or two of the names, the children in those categories swap seats. If you call 'Garden', all the children swap seats.

- In the popular game of **Duck, duck, goose**, these names can be substituted for more suitable ones, such as Bee and Wasp.

- **The giant's garden** is a popular game with the children. Prior to playing, the children cut out and paint large card flowers. You will need about twenty-seven altogether. The children sit in a circle. A child is chosen to be the giant and kneels in the centre of the circle, wearing a blindfold. The flowers are scattered around the inside of the circle. Two children are chosen to enter the circle and collect the flowers as quietly as they can. The 'giant' must listen carefully to try and ascertain their whereabouts and tag them. Once a child is tagged, they must stop collecting flowers and return to their seat. When both children have been tagged, or all the flowers have been collected, each child counts how many flowers they have.

- **Who's that animal?** is a guessing game. The children stand in a circle. They each think of an animal that might be in their garden that makes a noise, such as a cat, a dog or a bee. A child is chosen to stand in the centre and wear a blindfold. The remaining children walk around in a clockwise direction. The child in the centre calls 'Stop' and raises an arm to point to a child in the circle. This child makes their animal noise and the child in the centre has two attempts to guess which child it is.

- The game **What am I?** can be played using items from a garden (see page 22), although it is a good idea to show the children all the pictures prior to playing and discuss suitable questions they could ask.

- Another popular game is **Who can think of something _____?** You can name different categories, such as soft, prickly, that smells nice, hard or shiny, and the children must think of suitable items in a garden.

- The children can complete sentence stems, such as, '**If I were a flower/vegetable/ animal in the garden, I would be _____ because _____.**'

- The children can play an activity using the template of a garden gate (see page 120) photocopied on to A3 paper and folded in half to make a card. In pairs, the children colour the gate on the front of their card and then write or draw items that could be found in a garden inside. Older children can work with another pair and take turns to guess items inside their card. With younger children, it is better for the group to sit in a circle and for all the children to be involved in trying to guess an item behind each pair's gate.

- Children enjoy listening to stories with key words that require actions. An example is detailed below:

  Key words

Sun	Stand up and make a round sun movement with arms
Rain	Raise arms and wiggle fingers to represent rain
Garden	Stand up, turn around and sit down
Flowers	Clap twice
Water	Stamp feet twice

Tell the children the key words and their associated actions. For younger children, just use three of the key words. Explain that you are going to tell them a story and, every time they hear the key words, they must perform the associated actions. Read the following story slowly, allowing pauses after the key words for the children to perform:

> One day, the <u>sun</u> was shining brightly on Sasha's <u>garden</u>. Sasha looked out of her window at the bright <u>flowers</u>. 'I do hope the <u>sun</u> is not too hot for my lovely <u>flowers</u>,' she thought. 'Perhaps I should give them some <u>water</u>.'
>
> Sasha went outside into the <u>garden</u>. Just then, a huge black cloud appeared overhead and it began to <u>rain</u> heavily. Sasha ran back indoors quickly. 'Oh my poor <u>flowers</u>,' she thought, as she looked out of the window into the <u>garden</u>. 'All that <u>water</u> from the heavy <u>rain</u> is giving them quite a battering.'
>
> When the <u>rain</u> stopped, Sasha went to look at her <u>flowers</u>. There were puddles of <u>water</u> all over the <u>garden</u>. The <u>flowers</u> looked very sad, but, just then, the <u>sun</u> came out again and dried up all the <u>water</u>.
>
> The <u>flowers</u> lifted up their beautiful heads. 'Hooray for the <u>sun</u>,' said Sasha. 'My <u>garden</u> is beautiful again!'

Art

You can create a really eye-catching display with the cumulative results of several weeks' work. For maximum effect, place a large table against a wall or in a corner, so that you can make use of the table and area above. Cover the table with a suitable cloth or paper to represent the ground.

- You can make a very attractive frieze by printing broccoli, cabbage and lettuce leaves to represent trees and bushes.

- Sponge or finger-paint cut-out leaf shapes in various shades of green to scatter on the 'ground'. You can also make larger leaves by tie-dyeing cotton squares green and then cutting them into leaf shapes.

- Create three-dimensional flowers in pots using the templates in the photocopiable resources section (see page 118) on stiff card. On the same page, you will find templates for birds and butterflies.

- The birds can be covered in scraps of bright fabric and sequins, and look particularly colourful with feather tails. These can be hung above the 'ground' display. An alternative is to create wings for the birds from either hand or foot prints.

- The butterflies can be cut from black sugar paper, using coloured tissue paper to create a stained-glass effect. These are best placed on a window to allow the light to shine through. If you have young children and think this might be too tricky for them to manage, they can splodge wet paint on the wings on one side of the shape, then fold the butterfly in half to create a symmetrical pattern.

- The children can use air-drying clay to make bugs, worms, snails and other small garden animals, and paint them during the following art session.

- Hedgehogs provide an attractive feature and can be created using a cone of brown paper, with two small feet attached underneath. Strips of fringed paper can be glued on to create the spikes. The addition of googly eyes gives the final touch.

- Googly eyes also enhance spiders made from painted egg-box sections with pipe cleaner legs. They can be hung on cotton or placed on a web made from string.

- Bright peg insects can be placed within the 'garden' by attaching the pegs to leaves.

- Once all the plants and animals have been assembled, the display is a real delight to the eye.

PSHE

A PSHE display can be incorporated easily into the garden theme.

- Put up a 'tree trunk', a large brown-painted card cylinder, against a wall and add twisted tissue paper branches.

- Cut out leaves and bright fruit to attach to the branches.

- Depending on your focus in this area, you can ask the children to complete suitable sentence stems. For example:

    'I like _____ .'

    'I am good at _____ .'

    'Something I am good at in class is _____ .'

    'I was kind when _____ .'

    'A kind group is_____ .'

- If this is done during circle time, one of the adults can act as a scribe and write down the children's comments. These can later be written on to the leaves and fruit and hung from the branches.

- You can add any other relevant messages to this display on clouds, birds or small animals around the base of the tree.

Science

You can include various science sessions under the general topic of 'gardens', depending on the time of year.

- In winter, when there is little to see outside, you could focus on indoor experiments to develop the children's investigative powers. For example, ask the children to taste a variety of foods from the garden (such as a carrot, an apple, a spring onion and a pear).

- Choose eight different foods and ask the children to see how many they can identify correctly when they are (a) wearing a blindfold and (b) wearing a blindfold *and* pinching their nostrils together to cut off their sense of smell.

The results should show that a sense of smell plays an important part in 'tasting' different foods and is far more sensitive than taste alone.

- You can also create your own pH indicator by boiling a red cabbage and using the resulting strained water. Try testing different substances to assess their acidity and alkalinity, such as lemon juice or bicarbonate of soda.

- A very popular investigation, using a small, soft animal toy, such as a mouse, involves the children finding the 'warmest bed' for 'little mouse' to sleep in. The children are put into three groups and pack identical boxes or bags with three different materials. These could be any of the following: straw, wool, polystyrene beads, shredded paper, dried leaves or bubble wrap. You then put three small, glass bottles containing hot water into each of the 'beds'. Take the temperature of the water before placing the bottles into the containers, and again after thirty minutes and an hour. See which bed keeps its water bottle the warmest and hence would make the cosiest bed for 'little mouse'. You can add to the interest of this experiment by asking the children to guess beforehand which 'bed' will be the warmest.

- Around Christmas time, the children can plant hyacinth bulbs to take home and watch them grow. If they decorate the plant pots, they can be Christmas presents for their parents.

- If you feature the theme of gardens during spring or summer, the children could be well occupied clearing and maintaining a patch of garden and planting seeds. They could investigate how plants need water and sunlight to grow by planting runner bean seeds in four small pots of compost. Two pots are placed on a windowsill and one is given water, but the other remains dry. (It is a good idea to ensure that the compost you use is very dry for the seeds that are being deprived of water. You can dry it on a tray in the oven or leave it for several days to dry in the air.) The remaining two pots are placed somewhere dark, such as a cupboard, and, once again, only one pot is watered.

- You can look at the structure of plants and demonstrate how plants 'drink' using celery. Choose some with plenty of leaves and select the four innermost stalks. Place three of the stalks in water coloured with different food dyes and the fourth in clear water to act as a control. The colour is 'sucked' up into the leaves and will begin to show after an hour or so. By the following morning, the colour change will be quite impressive.

- The children could also plant either a sunflower or runner bean seed in individual pots to see whose will grow the tallest.

- Growing cress seeds in different shapes is another activity the children will enjoy. You place a wad of kitchen roll on to a waterproof surface and soak it with water. Then put cookie cutters on to the wet kitchen roll and sprinkle cress seeds inside the shapes. Keep the kitchen roll moist by adding water, but not directly on to the seeds. When the cress is about 2 cm high, you can remove it from the cookie cutter.

- The children could also investigate the mini-beasts that live in a garden and maybe learn a little about the life history of birds or other garden animals.

- Watching the life cycle of the butterfly is a fascinating experience for children. You can obtain Small Tortoiseshell caterpillars from Worldwide Butterflies (www.wwb. co.uk) – and they are remarkably easy to keep. They can either be housed in an aquarium with a lid, or a large shoebox (cut out the sides and replace with clear cellophane; and punch air holes into the top). They feed on stinging nettles, which are always plentiful. The children can measure the caterpillars, see how they discard their skins as they grow, watch them pupate and eventually release the butterflies outdoors. This whole process takes only a few weeks to complete.

- Looking at camouflage is an interesting topic. You can collect a variety of coloured and patterned fabrics and take the children outside to look at which fabrics blend in with the surroundings. They vote on the fabric they think is best. You can then look at some photos of animals that use camouflage.

Drama

A 'garden' theme offers a wealth of ideas for drama.

- Young children especially will enjoy pretending to be the different animals in a garden, or being plants growing tall and strong. They could, for example, act out the task of squirrels collecting and burying nuts or the life cycle of a butterfly.

- They could mime a storm developing, waggling fingers for gentle rain and swaying to a breeze, then stamping loudly and clapping their hands for the thunder.

- They could also mime the effects of different weathers of the four seasons, such as rain, wind, snow, frost, sun or fog, imagining how an animal in the garden might behave in the different weather conditions.

- Each half-term, we choose a simple story for the children to listen to and subsequently act out. An example story is set out on page 114 in the resources section. If possible, make some suitable mouse masks with the children. You could, perhaps, arrange for the children to perform their plays to classes within the school or their parents, while an adult reads the text aloud. The children can learn simple dialogue if they want to.

Cooking

Although it may not be possible to incorporate the current theme into all the cooking sessions, there are some occasions when the product could reflect the focus.

- So, for example, you might use biscuit cutters in the shapes of animals, such as rabbits, or prepare and cook produce that the children have grown in the school garden for them to taste.

- Of course, butterfly cakes are fun to make. Or you could make 'snail sandwiches' by cutting the crusts from slices of bread, buttering one slice and adding the filling, then rolling the slice up and cutting it into sections. Each section can be placed on a sliver of carrot to represent a snail.

- If you make a sponge in a large tray, you could cut out squares and then halve these into triangles. Covered in green icing, on a suitable trunk or stem, they make ideal trees or shrubs. The children can even add cake decorations as flowers or fruit.

CHAPTER 12

Devising a suitable programme

The following section details the group's sessions over a thirteen-week term. This will give you a real feel for the timetable that we offer. This programme is for the autumn term and includes items for Christmas. I have used 'under the sea' as the theme, as, like 'gardens', this offers a wealth of creative ideas.

You can either choose to use the sessions as they stand or you may prefer to modify them to the particular needs of your group. The SEAL booklets 'New beginnings', 'Getting on and falling out' and 'Years 1 and 2 small group activities' have been used as a basis for the PSHE and some circle activities.

Some of the activities are more suited to children in Year 2 and beyond, and, where this is the case, I have included an alternative activity in italics for younger children. If it is possible, arrange with the class teachers to have a week at the end of a term, free of children, for your planning and preparation. During this time you will be able to write a programme for the following term, make your display boards ready for the new theme and prepare the various templates you need for art.

Preparation

In addition to the specific details given below, a box at the beginning of each week gives a prompt for the resources required for those sessions.

If this is your first term, you will need to prepare backgrounds for three displays. You will need a large background area for the 'booster' poster display with bright backing paper and a border. Think of a suitable, positive heading (ours is 'Sunflower Superstars'). If it is possible, take photographs of the children prior to starting and print one large image and two smaller images of each child.

Display the larger images on the 'booster' poster board alongside the children's names. You will need one of the smaller images for the target sheet and the remaining image for a place mat. You can prepare a target sheet for each child on A4 paper, with a heading 'My Target' and a photograph of the child underneath. If the sheets are then laminated, they can be used again and again with dry-wipe pens.

The two remaining boards are for your incentive scheme and PSHE display and need a suitable 'sea' background. If you are feeling creative, you can decorate the boards with tissue paper 'seaweed', card 'shells' and any other marine features.

Decide on the desired behaviour you want to promote, for example, being friendly, actively participating or being sensible, and think of a corresponding item, for example, 'friendly fish', 'joining-in jellyfish' or 'sensible starfish'. You can cut the items out of brightly coloured paper and then divide them into about twelve component parts for each child. Although it is labour intensive, if you laminate the parts, you can use them for many years to come. Over the years, we have created a selection of items to choose from, such as sensible snowmen, sensible snakes, friendly fish, reliable rockets and our manners garden (with sunflowers). Each item is displayed alongside a child's name. When you see the child behaving in the desired manner, you award them a piece of their item. We try to start completing the items in around the second or third week after half-term.

It is important to leave sufficient time to enable each child to enjoy their reward, especially if, for example, they are allowed to bring a friend from their class to a session. To avoid too much disruption, you should only include one friend at a time.

You can add a further dimension to this display by numbering the component parts. For example, with a display of 'jellyfish', a jellyfish body is displayed next to each child's name. The appendages of each jellyfish are numbered 1 to 10. Create ten large, numbered fish or rocks for the display and place the corresponding appendage under each fish or rock. Display a large number line of 1 to 10 underneath the display. Each time a child receives another part of their jellyfish, invite them to work out which number fish or rock they need to look under to find the next appendage to add to their jellyfish. Complete with two eyes to make up twelve parts.

For the PSHE display, we usually draw and photocopy items for the children to colour in during the term. These are added to the background along with the recorded statements that the children have made during our PSHE focus time. If you think that preparing this display is too labour intensive, you could find magazine pictures to cut out and put on the background instead.

You will also need to prepare a visual timetable (see page 123) for display alongside the four rules (see page 10) and a helper's rota. For the latter, laminate a list of the children's names and devise a means of showing who the two helpers are for the current day. We use two small sunflowers placed alongside the names to indicate who is helping.

When preparing an area for the art display, try to create a flat surface with a suitable surrounding wall area, such as a large table in a corner, giving you two walls on which to include the children's work.

For the 'under the sea' display, we draped blue material over the table and added large shells. We placed a treasure chest, created from a cardboard box, on the table.

On white card you need to draw around the following templates for each child (see pages 124 to 130):

- a diver and fish for the place mat
- a mackerel
- a flatfish
- a jellyfish
- a pirate boat and shark
- a parrot.

You will also need to cut pirate hats (two for each child) from black sugar paper.

It is really worthwhile spending time prior to the commencement of your group in order to be well prepared. You will have some tricky children to cope with and the first few weeks of a new group can be quite challenging. Do not despair if this is the case, as by half-term they should have settled into their new routine and the group will be developing its own positive identity.

You do not want to have to sort out the resources you require during a session, leaving the children unoccupied and unsupervised.

W E E K 1

Ensure that the room is set up before each session with a circle of chairs and timetable, rules and helper's rota displayed. Lay out a variety of toys around the room. During the first few weeks, the activities are repeated frequently to help the children feel safe and begin to settle in.

Monday	A4 paper, pencil crayons
Tuesday	A4 paper, diver, fish, paint
Wednesday	expression cards (see page 117), beanbag, magician's cloak, cauldron
Thursday	big picture, board games

M O N D A Y

The circle activities focus on taking turns, speaking out, trying something new, participating, watching and listening.

Once the children are seated, introduce the adults and explain what will be happening during the afternoon. Show them the visual timetable and explain the symbols. You do not want to overwhelm the children with too much information, but you can tell them that they will be engaged in a lot of enjoyable activities that will include having a drink and biscuit. They will have a time to play with the toys and each other during the afternoon and, to ensure that everyone has a good time, they need to observe the four rules displayed.

▓ Greeting

For the first half-term, you will need to teach the children a variety of greetings. Thereafter, the names of the children and adults go into a 'hat' and a different person is selected each day to choose the greeting.

Today, you will send a handshake and 'hello' around the circle from person to person.

▓ Counting

Each day, count together how many people are present and then a volunteer child will count on their own. After half-term, the child choosing the greeting can also do the counting.

▓ Circle activities

✳ ACTIVITY 1

Each child, in turn, completes the sentence stem 'My name is _____ and I like to _____', describing an activity they enjoy doing. The adults can model what to do first, for example, 'My name is Mrs Sonnet and I like to swim'. One of the adults scribes what the children say to display on the 'booster' poster.

✳ ACTIVITY 2

Play a game of 'under the sea' (like 'farmyard'). Tell the children that they are going to be thinking about 'under the sea' during the term. They will be making things in art and playing games on this topic. Ask the children to think of three animals that live in the sea, for example, a starfish, a shark and an octopus, and give the children and adults these animal names consecutively around the circle. Explain that you will call the names of one or two of the animals and the children in that category must swap seats. If you call 'under the sea', everyone has to swap seats.

✳ ACTIVITY 3

Play a game of 'Who can think of something _____?' Ask the children questions, for example, 'Who can think of something shiny/delicious/scary/soft/funny/tall/valuable/prickly/smelly?' and choose volunteers to answer.

▦ Designated activity

Normally, the designated activity would be cooking or gardening on a Monday. Throughout this section, I will be providing recipes for cooking. If you are working in the spring or summer terms, you can substitute some of the cooking plans for gardening sessions. As this is the first day, I have timetabled an activity that requires less organisation than cooking.

Give the children an A4 sheet of paper. Ask them to draw and colour in a picture of themselves doing their favourite activity. When they have finished, ask them to show their pictures to the other children. Can they find someone else who likes to do the same thing?

▦ Free play

Show the children the toys and activities they can use. You may have to allot times for very popular items. For example, our sand tray is always in demand and, as we limit the number of users to two at a time, each pair is allowed 5 to 10 minutes, depending on demand. You can use free-play time to talk or play with any shy or nervous child and encourage others to pair up. We do not put out board games during this time, as we found that children invariably cheated and argued about the results.

▦ Refreshments

It is a good idea to schedule the refreshments for about half an hour before the end of the session. Five minutes prior to this time, the children start to tidy up and put away all the toys. The two helpers and one of the adults prepare the table, laying out plates, cups, biscuits and drinks (you could offer a choice of milk or squash). When the children are seated, the helpers take round the drinks and biscuits. Encourage the children to use set speeches of 'Would you like a biscuit/milk/squash?' with the responses of 'Yes please' or 'No thank you', followed by a further 'Thank you' on receipt of the item. Allow around 10 to 15 minutes for refreshments.

▦ Wash up/story time

One of the adults supervises the two helpers to clear the table and wash and wipe up the utensils. The remaining children are seated (we have large, comfortable beanbags) for a short story. As a general guideline, select books from the Year 1 or Year 2 library.

▦ Clapping rhyme/song/goodbye

The day ends with either a clapping rhyme or song and a calming goodbye ritual. When there is time, you might include 'show and tell' and try to ensure this happens on at least two days a week. Children love to sing and will soon acquire their favourite songs that they request over and over again. Look for some simple songs – if you are not very musical, you may have a CD available that the children can join in with.

✳ GOODBYE RHYME

>   Roll your hands so quickly
>   Go fast and then go slow
>   Fold your arms and sit up straight
>   Because it's time to go

T U E S D A Y

The circle activities focus on taking turns, participating, speaking out and recognising emotion in themselves and others.

Look at the visual timetable together and remind the children of the four rules. Show them the prepared display board for the incentive scheme that you are operating this term. Explain how they can earn the component parts and what reward they will receive when they have completed their item.

▨ Greeting

Send a handshake and 'hello' around the circle.

▨ Counting

Count the people present and ask for a volunteer to count.

▨ Circle activities

✳ The children take turns to complete the sentence stem 'My favourite toy is _____.'

✳ Ask the children to show you a happy face. Ask for volunteers to tell you what makes them happy.

✳ Ask the children to show you what sort of face they would have if the following happened:

- Someone called them a nasty name.
- They had lost their homework.
- Someone broke their favourite toy.
- They were opening a birthday present.
- They came last in a running race.
- They had no one to play with.
- They could hear a strange noise when they were in bed.
- They had hurt their leg.
- They were going to Disneyland tomorrow.

✳ Play a game of 'under the sea' as yesterday.

▨ Designated activity: art

Make personalised place mats for the table. These are useful to have, as you can decide where the children sit during refreshment time if, for example, you want to separate children because they argue or misbehave together. (Old, men's shirts with the arms shortened make ideal painting overalls.)

Each child paints a piece of A4 paper blue for a sea background. They colour-in a diver, the seaweed and a fish (see page 124). Silver paint looks effective on the diver if you have any. The children can print a pattern on the fish using a length of dowel or the round end of a straw, and orange paint. When all the items are dry, glue the fish, diver and seaweed on to the blue background. Put the small photographic image of the child's face on to the diver, then laminate the place mats for use (we replace the place mats at the beginning of each academic year, using a different theme).

- **Free play**

- **Refreshments**

- **Wash up/story time**

- **Clapping rhyme/song/goodbye**

Use the goodbye rhyme from yesterday.

WEDNESDAY

The circle activities focus on participating, speaking out, trying something new and working cooperatively in a group.

Look at the visual timetable and remind the children of the rules and incentive scheme.

- **Greeting**

Send a handshake and 'hello' around the circle.

- **Counting**

- **Circle activities**

✳ The children complete the sentence stem 'If I was an animal in the sea, I would be a _____ because _____.'

✳ AFLOAT IN A BOAT

See page 23.

- **Designated activity: PSHE**

Enlarge the expression cards on page 117 and remove or cover the headings. Hold them up, one at a time, and ask the children what feeling each expression represents. Place the cards face down. Invite the children to take turns to pick up a card. Ask the child with the card 'What could make you feel like that?' and they must try and think of an appropriate situation. If they cannot, invite the other children to give suitable ideas.

✳ MAGICIAN'S CLOAK

If you have anything suitable, provide a cloak for the magician to wear. Choose a child to be the magician and another to be the apprentice. Use a container for a cauldron. Explain to the children that they are going to make a special potion that will make people happy. They must think of ingredients that they can use. You may need to give the children some ideas to start them off, for example, chocolate, jokes, flowers, a toy, sunshine or a film. If you have older children, they may be able to think of abstract ideas such as friendship. The children put up their hands to contribute. The 'magician' chooses a child to name an ingredient. The 'apprentice' mimes collecting the ingredient and places it into the cauldron. Continue like this until all the children have had a turn to contribute. The 'magician' stirs the ingredients together while you say:

    Stir it round and stir it thick
    Our magic spell will do the trick!

The 'magician' mimes offering everyone a drink of the potion. Ask the children to show you their happy faces.

- **Free play**

- **Refreshments**

- **Wash up/story time**

- **Clapping rhyme/song/goodbye**

Repeat the goodbye ritual from Monday.

T H U R S D A Y

The circle activities focus on watching and listening, speaking out, participating, trying something new and working cooperatively within a group.

Look at the visual timetable and remind the children of the rules and incentive scheme.

▧ Greeting

Send a handshake and 'hello' around the circle.

▧ Counting

▧ Circle activities

✳ Introduce the big picture (see page 25). Explain to the children that, starting next week, you will add two items each week. They must study the picture each week and see if they can find what you have added. Ask them to have a good look at the picture now.

✳ The children complete the sentence stem 'I am good at _____.' Give them some ideas to help them think of a suitable answer, for example, riding my bike, swimming or playing on my PlayStation. An adult scribes their answers to write up later on the 'booster' poster.

✳ ZOOM AND EEK

Explain to the children that they are going to pass a spoken 'zoom' around the circle from person to person and practise doing this. Tell the children that, if they say 'eek' instead, the action changes direction, for example, travelling around the circle from a clockwise direction to an anticlockwise direction. However, they are only allowed one 'eek' each. Play the game until the 'zoom' travels all the way around the circle without an 'eek'.

▧ Designated activity: group games

The children are divided into two groups and each group plays a board game with one of the adults. If you have twelve children, you may have difficulty obtaining board games for six, as many are designed for four players. However, you could make your own, and several examples are detailed below:

✳ BALLOON GAME

On an A4 sheet of paper, draw a simple picture that includes six balloons. Photocopy this so that you have six copies. Colour the balloons so that each sheet has the same six different colours. Laminate the sheets. You will also need to prepare and laminate six circles of each colour, the same size as the balloons. Prepare a die with the six colours that you have used for your balloons.

The children each have a picture sheet. They take turns to roll the die. They can pick up a circle of the colour shown on the die and place it over the corresponding balloon on their sheet. If they already have that colour, they do not take another circle. The game continues until one player has collected all their circles and covered all the balloons on their card.

✳ CAR GAME

You can also use the coloured die for another game. Prepare an A3 sheet of paper by dividing it into six equal rows in landscape view. Divide the rows into around fourteen segments. Laminate the sheet – this is the road. Prepare six cars (or any other objects) that match the colours on the die and that are small enough to fit on to a segment. Line the six cars up at one end of the road. Each child, in turn, guesses which car will be the 'fastest' and which car will be the 'slowest'. Make a note of their guesses. The children take turns to roll the die and move the matching car one segment forward. The winner is noted, but the game continues until the last car reaches the end. The children see who correctly chose the fastest and slowest cars.

✳ GOING SHOPPING

You will need to prepare forty-eight different food and drink items and laminate them. You then need to make and laminate six shopping lists, with eight different items on each list that correspond to some of the forty-eight you have already prepared. Each child is given a shopping list and all the items are placed, face down, in the middle of the table. The children take turns to pick up an item and give it to whoever has it on their shopping list. The game continues until one player has collected all of the items on their shopping list.

✳ HUNGRY MOUTH

Prepare and laminate forty-eight small cards. Forty-two of the cards have apples on them and six have large 'hungry mouths'. Shuffle the cards and place them face down on a table. The children take turns to pick up a card. If they select an apple, they keep it. If they pick up a hungry mouth, they must put all of their apples back, face down, on the table. The hungry mouths are set aside once they have been picked up. The game continues until all of the cards have been picked up. The players count their apples to see who has the most.

You can also make and laminate games such as snakes and ladders or ludo, if funds are short.

Generally, the children can concentrate for two games before free play.

■ **Free play**

■ **Refreshments**

■ **Wash up/story time**

■ **Clapping rhyme/song/goodbye**
Repeat the goodbye ritual from yesterday.

WEEK 2

Monday	beanbag, ingredients and utensils for cooking
Tuesday	beanbag, small toy for hiding, jellyfish (see page 126), scissors, thin strips of coloured tissue paper, glue and stickers, paint
Wednesday	beanbag, photographs, two beakers of water, two eggs, salt
Thursday	beanbag, big picture, animal pictures, skittles and balls

M O N D A Y

The circle activities focus on trying something new, participating, speaking out and working cooperatively with a partner.

Look at the visual timetable and remind the children of the rules and incentive scheme.

■ **Greeting**
Choose a child who is sitting well to stand in the centre of the circle. They throw a beanbag to each child and adult around the circle and say 'Hello _____'. The beanbag is returned each time with a reciprocal 'Hello _____'.

▨ Counting

▨ Circle activities

✳ The children complete the sentence stem 'One thing I like to do with my friends is _____.'

✳ Play a game of categories. If any child is included in the category you call, they swap seats. For example:

- Anyone who has a brother/sister/dog/rabbit.
- Anyone who likes chocolate/chips/Brussel sprouts.
- Anyone with brown hair/blue eyes/white socks.

✳ Put the children into pairs. Ask them to find one thing their partner likes to eat and one thing they both dislike to eat. The children report their partners' likes and dislikes back to the circle. If they have forgotten, their partner can whisper in their ear.

▨ Designated activity: cooking

Write up the recipe below for the children to see. Place a bowl of warm water, soap and a towel on a suitable surface and ask each child to wash their hands. Ideally, you will need enough bowls and utensils for each set to be shared by a maximum of three children. You may be able to persuade a kind parent to make aprons (we did) or perhaps the PTA would provide funds to buy some.

The children stand around a table, three to a bowl. Tell them that today they are going to make small cakes. Read through the recipe with them, asking if they know what each of the ingredients is:

- 100 g soft margarine
- 100 g caster sugar
- 1 egg
- 150 g self-raising flour

Put the margarine and sugar into each bowl. (If you put in the margarine, the children can each add one ingredient to the bowl.) The children take turns to cream them together. When the mixture is ready, add the egg and mix further. Finally, add the flour and mix well together. The children take turns to spoon the mixture into cake cases.

Bake in an oven at Gas Mark 6 or 200° C (400° F) for ten to fifteen minutes. Allow the cakes to cool on a wire rack. There should be a sufficient number to last for two days.

▨ Free play

▨ Refreshments

▨ Wash up/story time

▨ Clapping rhyme/song/goodbye

✳ GOODBYE RITUAL

Each child, in turn, completes the sentence stem 'One thing I enjoyed today was _____.'

TUESDAY

The circle activities focus on watching and listening, taking turns and working cooperatively within a group.

Look at the visual timetable together and remind the children of the rules and incentive scheme.

▓ Greeting

Choose a child who is sitting well to do the beanbag greeting as yesterday.

▓ Counting

▓ Circle activities

✳ HUNT THE SMALL TOY

Using a tick list of names, choose two different children each week to hide and search for a small toy (we use a small plastic dog). One of the children leaves the room with an adult while the other child hides the toy within the room. The rest of the group guide the seeker with cries of 'cold', 'warmer', 'hotter' and 'scorching!' to the toy's location. The roles are then reversed between the two children.

✳ Send a smile from person to person around the circle. Ask the children, 'Who would like to start the smile?' When the action has travelled around the circle, ask the child, 'Has your smile come back to you yet?' Repeat with other children.

✳ Play a game of 'under the sea'.

▓ Designated activity: art

Prior to the session, you will need to cut thin strips from brightly coloured tissue paper. The children glue tissue paper strips to the inside of one half of their jellyfish. They paint the outside of both halves the same bright colour. When the paint is dry, staple the two halves together and hang the jellyfish above the art table.

▓ Free play

▓ Refreshments

▓ Wash up/story time

▓ Clapping rhyme/song/goodbye

Complete the same sentence stem as yesterday.

WEDNESDAY

The circle activities focus on the children recognising emotion in themselves and others, speaking out, trying something new and participating.

Look at the visual timetable together and remind the children of the rules and incentive scheme.

▓ Greeting

Choose a child who is sitting well to do the beanbag greeting as yesterday.

▓ Counting

▓ Circle activities

Choose three or four photographs from the SEAL resources pack. Ask the children to look at each photograph in turn. Ask them to describe what they think is happening. How does the child in the photograph feel? Ask them to think of a situation when they have felt the same. Finish with a 'happy' photograph. The children complete the sentence stem 'I was happy when _____.'

✳ FISH IN THE SEA

The children stand in a circle, facing in a clockwise direction. You call out various categories and the children have to move accordingly:

- Low tide: walk forward slowly.
- High tide: walk forward quickly.
- Tide turns: change direction.
- Trawlers: about-crawl on hands and knees to avoid nets.
- Sharks ahead: walk carefully backwards.
- Coral reef: jump forwards.

▨ Designated activity: science

You will need two identical large beakers, two eggs and salt. The children can sit around the table you are working on. Fill the beakers two-thirds with water and place them on the table. Ask the children if they can think of a difference between seawater and river water. Give them prompts until they come up with the answer that seawater is salty. Tell them that seawater is more buoyant because it is salty. This means it is easier to float in seawater. In fact, there is a sea in Israel – the Dead Sea – where you cannot sink. You are going to prove this with their help. Tell the children you have two beakers of tap water. Place an egg in the first beaker and watch it sink to the bottom. Ask for volunteers to put salt into the second beaker until the egg floats. Did it take much salt to do this?

▨ Free play

▨ Refreshments

▨ Wash up/story time

▨ Clapping rhyme/song/goodbye

Complete the sentence stem as yesterday.

T H U R S D A Y

The circle activities focus on watching and listening, speaking out, trying something new and participating.

Look at the visual timetable together and remind the children of the rules and incentive scheme.

▨ Greeting

Choose a child who is sitting well to do the beanbag greeting as yesterday.

▨ Counting

▨ Circle activities

✳ Ask the children to look at the big picture to see if they can find what you have added. Allow each child, in turn, to guess. Let the children have two guesses before telling them, if they haven't found the additions. You will be able to judge, after a few weeks, if what you are adding is too difficult, too easy or just right.

✳ WHAT AM I? (YEAR 2+)

See page 22.

✳ AFLOAT IN A BOAT

See page 23.

Designated activity: group game

SKITTLES

We use painted, plastic squash bottles. Make a list of the children's names on the board. Arrange the chairs in a row along one side of the skittle 'alley', so that the children can sit and watch the action until it is their turn. Call each child to throw three balls at the skittles and note down their scores. Allow younger children to stand closer to the skittles. We generally have two rounds.

Free play

Refreshments

Wash up/story time

Clapping rhyme/song/goodbye

Complete the sentence stem as yesterday.

WEEK 3

Monday	two telephones, expression cards, ingredients and utensils for cooking
Tuesday	two telephones, small toy, large die, mackerels (see page 127), scissors, squares of material, dowels or plasticine, glue and stickers
Wednesday	two telephones, magician's cloak, cauldron
Thursday	two telephones, big picture, targets

MONDAY

The circle activities focus on participating, working cooperatively within a group, the children recognising emotion in themselves and others and speaking out.

From now on, the children will be getting used to the timetable so you do not have to look at it every day. Remind them of the rules and incentive scheme just at the beginning of each week.

Greeting

✳ RING, RING TELEPHONE

The children take turns around the circle to hold two telephones and call someone up. Everyone sings or says the chant:

Ring, ring, telephone who is there?

_____ is calling _____

[the child chooses someone in the circle to hand the second phone to], can you hear?

Pick up the telephone and hear them say:

'Hello _____, have a good day.' [This is said by the child whose turn it is.]

Counting

Circle activities

✳ SEND A SMILE (see page 58)

Place the expression cards (see page 117) face up. Tell the children a variety of situations and ask for volunteers to choose a suitable expression to go with each situation. Is there more than one choice?

EXAMPLES

- Your best friend cannot come round to play.
- It is your favourite lesson.
- It is raining and you can't go out.
- You do not know how to do your work.
- There is a scary film on the television.
- Someone has taken your new toy.

✳ The children complete the sentence stem 'I am excited when _____.'

Designated activity: cooking

PIZZA

It is a good idea to canvass the children's likes for pizza toppings during the previous week. Choose three or four, for example, ham, cheese, salami and pineapple. You can either use large pizza bases cut into segments, or small bases cut in half. The children wash their hands. Under supervision, the children can cut up the ingredients and grate the cheese. They spread their pizza section with tomato paste and then add the desired toppings.

Cook the pizzas according to the instructions on the pizza base packaging. Allow the pizzas to cool slightly, but serve them warm at refreshment time (you may have to delay putting the pizzas into the oven so that you time this correctly).

Free play

Refreshments

Wash up/story time

Clapping rhyme/song/goodbye

✳ GOODBYE RITUAL

Sing to each child, 'Goodbye _____, have a good home-time.'

T U E S D A Y

The circle activities focus on watching and listening, working cooperatively, trying something new, participating and taking turns.

Greeting

Repeat ring, ring telephone as yesterday.

Counting

Circle activities

✳ HUNT THE SMALL TOY
See page 58.

✳ ZOOM AND EEK
See page 55.

✳ Number the children and adults 1 to 5 consecutively around the circle. Roll a large die. The players with the number shown swap places. If a number 6 turns up, everyone swaps places.

▨ Designated activity: art

Prior to the lesson, you will need to cut out small squares of a suitable material, grey or silver if possible. Each child has a mackerel to cut out and glue material on to for the art table (write the child's name in pencil on the back of their fish).

The fish look very effective if you can display them in a raised position from the 'seabed'. We attach them to thin dowel, pushed into custom-made bases, but you could use plasticine bases.

▨ Free play

▨ Refreshments

▨ Wash up/story time

▨ Clapping rhyme/song/goodbye

Sing goodbye to each child as yesterday.

W E D N E S D A Y

The circle activities focus on trying something new, participating, taking turns and speaking out.

▨ Greeting

Repeat ring, ring telephone as yesterday.

▨ Counting

▨ Circle activities

✳ SEND A SQUEEZE

The children and adults hold hands around the circle. Send a gentle hand squeeze from person to person. Ask the children if anyone would like to start the squeeze. Ask them to tell you when their squeeze arrives back to them.

✳ WHO CAN THINK OF SOMETHING?

See page 52.

✳ UNDER THE SEA

See page 52.

▨ Designated activity: PSHE

✳ MAGICIAN'S CLOAK (See page 54)

Make a spell for a kind group. What ingredients could the children put into the cauldron? Give some examples, for example, a smile, friendliness, helping and sharing. Put the children into pairs to think what a kind group might look like.

Younger children will need a lot of prompting for ideas, such as children playing nicely together, children sharing, taking turns, helping others and speaking politely. An adult writes up the children's comments for the PSHE display.

▨ Free play

▨ Refreshments

■ **Wash up/story time**

■ **Clapping rhyme/song/goodbye**

Sing goodbye to each child as yesterday.

T H U R S D A Y

The circle activities focus on watching and listening, participating, working cooperatively, taking turns, speaking out and using expressive language.

■ **Greeting**

Repeat ring, ring telephone as yesterday.

■ **Circle activities**

✳ THE BIG PICTURE

See page 25.

✳ SEND A SMILE

See page 58.

✳ Children take turns to start the smile off.

✳ Ask for volunteers to say what they like about several of the children. You may need to give them some ideas. For example:

'_____ is kind',

'_____ has a nice smile',

'_____ shares toys with me', or

'_____ makes me laugh'.

An adult scribes to add the comments to the 'booster' poster in speech bubbles. Repeat this process each day until you have positive comments about all of the children.

■ **Designated activity: group game**

✳ TARGET PRACTICE

You can create targets from six large flowerpots or cardboard boxes. Place three in the front, worth five points each; two behind these, worth ten points each; and one at the back, worth twenty points. Make a list of the children's names on the board.

The children arrange their chairs alongside the throwing 'alley'.

Each child, in turn, tries to throw three beanbags into the target containers. Record the scores on the board.

Play two rounds of the game. If you have any funding, you can buy purpose-made target mats or nets.

■ **Free play**

■ **Refreshments**

■ **Wash up/story time**

■ **Clapping rhyme/song/goodbye**

Sing goodbye to each child as yesterday.

W E E K 4

Monday	noisy object, blindfold, ingredients and utensils for cooking
Tuesday	small toy, clay and utensils
Wednesday	beanbag, animal pictures, 2 litre squash bottle, darning needle, bowl
Thursday	big picture, large die, puppet or photograph, parachute or items for team games

M O N D A Y

The circle activities focus on trying something new, participating, taking turns and speaking out.

Remind the children of the rules and incentive scheme.

▨ Greeting

The children stand in front of their chairs in a circle. One child begins the action by crossing the circle to greet a second child. They can do this by shaking hands, giving 'high fives', bowing or any other recognised form of greeting. The first child then sits down. The second child repeats the process and the activity continues until all but one of the participants is seated. This person says 'Hello everyone', before sitting down.

▨ Counting

▨ Circle activities

✳ Send a smile from child to child around the circle. Ask who wants to start the smile off on its journey.

✳ Prior to the session, write the following statements on to a board:

I belong.
I am special.
I am kind.
I can work hard.
I make people happy.
I can think about others.
I am calm and happy.
I can manage my anger.

Go through the statements with the children.

Ask each child to choose the statement that they think suits them best. It does not matter if several children choose the same statement.

✳ Play a game of 'dragon's den'. You will need something noisy, such as a hand-held percussion instrument with bells, and a blindfold. A child is chosen to be the dragon, puts on the blindfold and crouches down in the centre of the circle. The noisy object is placed on the floor next to them.

✳ Everyone says the rhyme:

Look at the dragon resting his/her head
Look at the treasure close to his/her bed
See the brave warrior enter the den
Capture the treasure and creep out again.

During this chant, you indicate to a child to enter the circle as quietly as possible and take the treasure. All the children put their hands behind their backs. The dragon takes off the blindfold and tries to guess the identity of the 'warrior'. They are allowed two guesses. Repeat several times.

▦ Designated activity: cooking
Write up the recipe below for chocolate-chip cookies. All children wash their hands and stand three to a bowl around the work table.

- 100 g soft margarine
- 100 g caster sugar
- 1 medium egg
- 200 g plain flour
- chocolate-chips

Weigh out and cream together the margarine and sugar. Beat in the egg and add the flour. Finally, add the chocolate-chips. The children spoon small amounts on to a baking tray covered with greaseproof paper.

Bake at Gas Mark 5 or 190º C (375º F) for approximately ten minutes until the biscuits are golden. Cool on a wire rack.

▦ Free play

▦ Refreshments

▦ Wash up/story time

▦ Clapping rhyme/song/goodbye

✳ GOODBYE RITUAL

Say the following to the children:

Our day is nearly over and soon we will be done.
We've worked and played together and we've had lots of fun.
There is just time before we go and skip and walk and run,
To look round at our friends and say 'goodbye' to everyone.

The children say their goodbyes.

TUESDAY

The circle activities focus on working cooperatively within a group, taking turns and speaking out.

▦ Greeting
Stand and greet as yesterday.

▦ Counting

▦ Circle activities

✳ HUNT THE SMALL TOY
See page 58.

✳ ZOOM AND EEK
See page 55.

✳ Ask the children to think of something about themselves that they would like others to know. Tell them the information they give will be put on to the 'booster' poster. It could be something they have, something they like or something they do. An adult scribes their statements.

▨ Designated activity: art

The children make 'treasure' from air-drying clay. They roll out the clay and cut out coins using circle cutters. They can use a variety of objects to stamp patterns on the coins. They can also make jewellery.

▨ Free play

▨ Refreshments

▨ Wash up/story time

▨ Clapping rhyme/song/goodbye

Repeat the goodbye ritual as yesterday.

W E D N E S D A Y

The circle activities focus on participating, working cooperatively within a group, taking turns and speaking out.

▨ Greeting

Stand and greet as yesterday.

▨ Counting

▨ Circle activities

✳ SEND A SQUEEZE
  See page 62.

✳ AFLOAT IN A BOAT
  See page 23.

✳ WHAT AM I? (YEAR 2+)
  See page 22.

✳ *The children complete the sentence stem 'My favourite TV programme is _____.'*

▨ Designated activity: science

Take an empty 2 litre fizzy drink bottle and pierce a series of holes with a darning needle (do not make them too big) around the circumference, approximately 7 cm from the base. Fill the bottle with water and screw on the top firmly. Stand the bottle in a container, placed on a table. Ask the children to gather round. Tell them you are going to do a little magic. Unscrew the lid. Air enters the bottle and the air pressure pushes water out of the holes. Screw up the lid and the water stops flowing. Let all the children have a go at 'making magic'.

Ask the children if they can think what is happening. What is going into the bottle when you unscrew the lid? If they do not know, ask what is all around them. If they do not know this, use something such as a newspaper to create a waft of air on all the children. Continue until you have established that air pushes the water out of the bottle.

■ **Free play**

■ **Refreshments**

■ **Wash up/story time**

■ **Clapping rhyme/song/goodbye**

Repeat the goodbye ritual as yesterday.

T H U R S D A Y

The circle activities focus on participating, watching and listening, and speaking out.

■ **Greeting**

Stand and greet as yesterday.

■ **Counting**

■ **Circle activities**

✳ Look at the big picture with two new additions.

✳ THE DIE GAME

See page 62.

✳ Using a puppet or a picture of a child with a sad face, tell the children that the 'character' has just been told they are going to a new school. Ask the children how the character might be feeling. When they respond with 'sad', ask them why. Establish that the character will miss their friends. How will they feel when they start the new school (nervous, lonely, and so on)?

✳ Ask the children how they could help a child who was new to their school – perhaps by being kind and friendly. How would they be kind and friendly?

■ **Designated activity: parachute games**

If you can, try to obtain a small parachute, designed for twelve players. A large parachute is too weighty for a small group to handle. If you do not have a suitable parachute, you can play team games instead. Put the children into two teams and play games such as passing the ball along, behind their backs, over their heads, between their legs and by bouncing. The children can also walk while balancing beanbags on their heads or large balls between their knees. Use an old curtain or duvet cover and place a large, soft ball on top. The teams stand on either side of the curtain and try to shake the ball off on the opposing team's side.

■ **Free play**

■ **Refreshments**

■ **Wash up/story time**

■ **Clapping rhyme/song/goodbye**

Repeat the goodbye ritual as yesterday.

W E E K 5

Monday	storyboard or photograph, large die, ingredients and utensils for cooking
Tuesday	small toy, everyday objects, paint
Wednesday	button and key, blindfold, magician's cloak, cauldron, items for 'giving instructions'
Thursday	big picture, board games

M O N D A Y

The circle activities focus on trying something new, participating, watching and listening, the children recognising emotion in themselves and others, expressing feelings appropriately, taking turns and speaking out.

▧ Greeting

✳ CLAP AND CALL

One child begins the action by saying 'Hello _____' to another child. Everyone claps twice and then the second child calls hello to a third child, followed by two claps, and so on. The aim of the activity is to create a flowing action of clapping and calling (not as easy as it sounds with some children). People can be named more than once. Continue the action for several minutes.

▧ Counting

▧ Circle activities

✳ IN THE DRIVING SEAT

While remaining seated, children mime being in different seats, for example, driving a car, playing the piano, riding a horse (rock for walking, bounce up and down for trotting and move vigorously for galloping), swinging on a swing, driving a motorbike and, to finish, riding on a roller coaster (the children's favourite). For this, the children mime locking themselves into their seat. They pretend to hold the bar in front of them and slowly raise their hands above their head and lean back as you talk them through going up a steep incline, building the tension as you go. At the top, they wait until you say 'and down!' The children all squeal and rapidly bring their hands down to the floor – great fun!

✳ Using a storyboard or photograph from the SEAL resource pack, look at a situation where a child is sad. Ask the children how the child in the photograph is feeling. How can they tell? What might have made him feel this way? What could make him feel better?

✳ Ask the children to show you how their faces might look if they were on a real roller coaster. What about being on a ghost train or a roundabout, or eating candyfloss, for example?

✳THE DIE GAME

See page 62.

▨ Designated activity: cooking

MAKING SANDWICHES

Prior to the session, canvass children on their preferred sandwich fillers and bring in three or four. You will need a white and brown loaf, butter or vegetable oil spread, and cling film.

Ask the children to wash their hands. Under supervision, they can prepare the fillings, for example, grate the cheese (be careful of scraped fingers) or chop the tomatoes (again with care).

Each child takes two slices of bread, butters them, adds their chosen filler and makes their sandwich. They can cut the crusts off if they like and cut their sandwich into halves or quarters. They wrap their sandwich in cling film to eat at refreshment time.

▨ Free play

▨ Refreshments

▨ Wash up/story time

▨ Clapping rhyme/song/goodbye

✳ GOODBYE RITUAL

Say to the children:

> Sit on the floor as quiet as can be,
> As calm as a meadow and as still as a tree.
> Put your hands in your lap, rest them there just so,
> Now you have shown you are ready to go.

TUESDAY

The circle activities focus on working cooperatively within a group, taking turns, watching and listening, and using expressive language.

▨ Greeting

Clap and call as yesterday.

▨ Counting

▨ Circle activities

✳ HUNT THE SMALL TOY
  See page 58.

✳ MY OBJECT
  See page 22 (Year 2+).

✳ WHAT COULD I TAKE TO THE PARTY?
  See page 23.

* WALKING A TIGHTROPE

Clear away the chairs. The children line up behind you and follow you across the room. You mime walking on different surfaces for them to copy, for example, walking on a tightrope, walking on hot coals, jumping on stepping stones across a river, wading through thick squelchy mud, skating across ice, tiptoeing on a noisy marble floor to escape a giant, and walking on the moon.

▓ Designated activity: art

The children paint the clay treasure they made last week. If you can, use gold and silver paint, as this is most effective. Once the artwork is dry, arrange the coins in and around the treasure chest on your display.

▓ Free play

▓ Refreshments

▓ Wash up/story time

▓ Clapping rhyme/song/goodbye

Repeat the goodbye ritual as yesterday.

WEDNESDAY

The circle activities focus on working cooperatively within a group, participating and taking turns.

▓ Greeting

Clap and call as yesterday.

▓ Counting

▓ Circle activities

* SEND A SMILE

See page 58.

* BUTTON AND KEY

See page 21.

* GIVING INSTRUCTIONS

See page 20.

▓ Designated activity: PSHE

Push back the chairs to create a large space. Ask the children to show you how they would look and how they would walk if they were feeling happy, sad, frightened, angry, lonely and excited. Ask for volunteers to model looking and walking in a particular mood for the others to guess.

Put the children into pairs. Ask them to tell their partner one kind thing they have done this week. The children bring their chairs back to the circle. They each tell the group about the kind deed their partner has done. If they forget, their partner can whisper in their ear to remind them. An adult scribes the kind deeds to add to the PSHE display.

* MAGICIAN'S CLOAK

Choose a magician and apprentice to collect all of the kind deeds from the children and put into their cauldron. They mix up the ingredients while everyone says, 'Stir it round and stir it thick, our magic spell will do the trick.'

The magician mimes sprinkling each child with the magic kindness.

- **Free play**

- **Refreshments**

- **Wash up/story time**

- **Clapping rhyme/song/goodbye**
Repeat the goodbye ritual as yesterday.

T H U R S D A Y

The circle activities focus on watching and listening, taking turns and participating.

▨ Greeting
Clap and call as yesterday.

▨ Counting

▨ Circle activities

✳ THE BIG PICTURE
See page 25.

✳ Ask the children if they remember the character you introduced last week who was starting a new school. Show them the character. Ask if they can remember what they should do to help someone who was new to their school. What might they need to know to get on in their new school? Establish that the character would need to know the school rules. Ask the children if they know why a school has rules. Look at the group's rules to see why they are important. Establish that they are to keep people safe and happy and to protect property.

✳ RABBIT'S EARS
See page 24.

▨ Designated activity: group game
The children play board games with the adults.

▨ Free play

▨ Refreshments

▨ Wash up/story time

▨ Clapping rhyme/song/goodbye
Repeat the goodbye ritual as yesterday.

WEEK 6

Monday	expression cards, ingredients and utensils for cooking
Tuesday	small toy, animal pictures, flatfish (see page 127), scissors, tissue paper, glue and stickers, large piece of cardboard, paint
Wednesday	button and key, blindfold, 'camouflage' materials
Thursday	big picture, noisy object, blindfold, painted backdrop

MONDAY

The circle activities focus on participating, watching and listening, the children recognising emotion in themselves and others, taking turns and working cooperatively within a group.

▦ Greeting

✳ WHO IS CALLING?

The children stand in a circle. Choose a child (A) to begin the action. Say the chant and clap to the rhythm:

Who is [A] calling? Listen out with care.
[A] is calling _____ [A names B], then sits down on his/her chair [A sits].

The chant continues with B and so on until one person is left standing. They say hello to everyone.

▦ Counting

▦ Circle activities

✳ CATEGORIES

Call different categories and children change seats if they are in the named category.

✳ Put out the expression cards face down. Invite each child to turn one over. Ask the child what might make them feel like that? If they have trouble thinking of a suitable situation, the other children can give them ideas.

✳ RABBIT'S EARS

See page 24.

▦ Designated activity: cooking

✳ FRUITY BUNS

• 110 g self-raising flour	• 50 g caster sugar	• 25 g raspberry jam
• 50 g margarine	• 1/2 egg	

Pre-heat the oven to Gas Mark 6 or 200° C (400° F). Grease two baking sheets.

Put the flour into each bowl and cut the margarine into small chunks. Add the chunks of margarine to the bowl. The children take turns to rub the margarine into the flour with their fingertips until the mixture resembles fine breadcrumbs. Add the egg to the mixture and work into a dough. Cover the work surface with a sprinkling of flour and give each child a small piece of dough. The children roll the dough into a ball and make a dent in the middle of each bun. They fill the dent with a teaspoon of jam and place the buns on a baking tray. Cook for around ten minutes until the buns have risen and turned golden. Cool on a wire rack.

▦ **Free play**

▦ **Refreshments**

▦ **Wash up/story time**

▦ **Clapping rhyme/song/goodbye**

✳ GOODBYE RITUAL

Say to the children:

> We are sitting quietly to show that we all know
> That it is our home-time and we're ready to go.
> We are waiting quietly for (name of adult) to say
> 'Goodbye children, we've had a lovely day.'

T U E S D A Y

The circle activities focus on working cooperatively within a group, taking turns, speaking out, and watching and listening.

▦ **Greeting**

Repeat 'who is calling?' as yesterday.

▦ **Counting**

▦ **Circle activities**

✳ HUNT THE SMALL TOY

See page 58.

✳ WHAT AM I? (YEAR 2+)

See page 22.

✳ *The children complete the sentence stem 'My favourite dinner is _____.'*

✳ FISH IN THE SEA

See page 59.

▦ **Designated activity: art**

The children cut out a flatfish and glue scrunched-up pieces of tissue paper on to one side of the fish. You can either use bright colours or find a colour that is close to the table cover on your display (to demonstrate camouflage). Encourage them to use small pieces of tissue paper, as this will give a better finish.

While the children are doing this, call two at a time to paint a backdrop for your drama session on Thursday. You will need a large piece of cardboard, or several pieces joined together. Paint the top half blue, to represent the sea, and the bottom half yellow, for the sand.

▦ **Free play**

▦ **Refreshments**

▦ **Wash up/story time**

▦ **Clapping rhyme/song/goodbye**

Repeat the goodbye ritual as yesterday.

W E D N E S D A Y

The circle activities focus on working cooperatively within a group, participating, taking turns and speaking out.

▓ Greeting

Repeat 'who is calling?' as yesterday.

▓ Counting

▓ Circle activities

✳ SEND A SQUEEZE

See page 62.

✳ Remind the children of the 'character' you introduced who went to a new school. Explain that they have been in trouble. This is what they did:

- On Monday, they took an apple from the fruit basket during literacy and started to eat it. When should they have eaten it?
- On Tuesday, they broke a pencil in half because they could not do their sums. What should they have done?
- On Wednesday they talked in assembly. When do you have to be quiet in school?
- On Thursday they called someone a nasty name in the playground. Why was this wrong?
- On Friday, they played nicely with a classmate who was feeling lonely. Was this a good thing to do?

✳ BUTTON AND KEY

See page 21.

▓ Designated activity: science

Prior to the lesson, try to find some photos of well-camouflaged fish. Prepare a board covered in a material that has a small pattern. Cut out squares of various other materials. Try to choose some that are different and others that are similar to the background material. Show the children the photographs. Ask if they have ever heard of the word 'camouflage'. Explain in simple terms what this means, that is the animals use their colouring to blend into their background. Why might they do this? Suggest that the reason might be to hide from predators.

Show the children the prepared board. Explain that you have a set of different materials. Tell them you need their help in choosing the material that would provide the best camouflage. Pin each square, in turn, on to the background. Ask each time 'Is this one good?' When you have finished, take a vote on the best.

If you would prefer to conduct this experiment outside, you could ask the children which of your chosen materials would blend in best with a particular surrounding.

▓ Free play

▓ Refreshments

▓ Wash up/story time

▓ Clapping rhyme/song/goodbye

Repeat the goodbye ritual as yesterday.

THURSDAY

The circle activities focus on working cooperatively within a group, participating, taking tu
watching and listening.

▨ Greeting

✳ WHO IS CALLING?

See page 72.

▨ Counting

▨ Circle activities

✳ THE BIG PICTURE

See page 25.

✳ PASS IT ALONG

See page 24.

✳ DRAGON'S DEN

See page 64.

▨ Designated activity: drama

Explain to the children that they are going to do some drama – they will pretend they are going to
the seaside.

- Put them into two or three family groups depending on number.
- Place the backdrop that you painted at one end of the room. This is their destination.
- Place a row of chairs, two at a time for the train. Their homes are at the other end of the room.
- Ask the children to decide who is in their family group – a mother, a father, a big brother, children, a grandparent, and so on.
- Ask them to tell you all the things they will need to take for a day at the seaside – a picnic, a bucket and spade, swimming costumes and towels, a blanket to sit on, and so on.
- They mime preparing their picnic and packing their items.
- Ask them what they have included in their picnic to eat and drink.
- When they are ready, one family boards the train. The other groups wait to join the train at station stops.
- Ask what they can see out of the train windows.
- Talk them through the journey.

When they reach their destination, they leave the train and mime carrying their belongings to the
beach. What will they do there? They can mime eating their picnic, building sandcastles, splashing
in the sea, looking in rock pools, eating an ice cream, and so on.

They then pack away their belongings and make the return journey home.

Ask them what was the best bit of their day at the seaside.

▨ Free play

▨ Refreshments

▨ Wash up/story time

▨ Clapping rhyme/song/goodbye

Repeat the goodbye ritual as yesterday.

HALF-TERM

You should now have enough knowledge of the children to prepare their individual target sheets. During the next half-term, each child should complete the incentive scheme and enjoy the reward that is offered.

The children can take turns to choose the greeting and count how many people are present and you can choose a goodbye ritual from the selection learned or any others that you might know.

WEEK 7

Monday	magician's cloak, cauldron, noisy object, blindfold, ingredients and utensils for cooking
Tuesday	small toy, items for 'giving instructions', boxes, paint, boats and sharks (see page 128), paper straws, glue and stickers, felt-tip pens
Wednesday	N/A
Thursday	big picture, board games

Remind children of the rules and the incentive scheme.

MONDAY

The circle activities focus on working cooperatively within a group, participating, taking turns and speaking out.

■ **Greeting**

■ **Counting**

■ **Circle activities**

✳ SEND A SMILE
See page 58.

✳ MAGICIAN'S CLOAK
Make a potion to cheer somebody up (see page 54).

✳ DRAGON'S DEN
See page 64.

■ **Designated activity: cooking**

✳ CHOCOLATE-CHIP CAKES

Add chocolate-chips to small cake mixture (see page 57).

■ **Free play**

■ **Refreshments**

▨ **Wash up/story time**

▨ **Clapping rhyme/song/goodbye**

T U E S D A Y

The circle activities focus on working cooperatively within a group, taking turns, participating, listening and speaking out.

▨ **Greeting**

▨ **Counting**

▨ **Circle activities**

✳ HUNT THE SMALL TOY

See page 58.

✳ ZOOM AND EEK

See page 55.

✳ The children complete the sentence stem 'One thing I enjoyed doing in the holiday was
_____.'

✳ GIVING INSTRUCTIONS

See page 20.

▨ **Designated activity: art**

The children are going to start work on their pirate ship scenes. They need to paint the top half of the inside of their boxes blue to represent the sea. They then need to glue flattened paper straws to the hull of their ships on both sides (it is probably easier to trim the straws to the correct shape after the glue has dried). They also need to colour the sails for their ships and the sharks.

▨ **Free play**

▨ **Refreshments**

▨ **Wash up/story time**

▨ **Clapping rhyme/song/goodbye**

W E D N E S D A Y

The circle activities focus on working cooperatively within a group, participating, watching and listening, speaking out and taking turns.

▨ **Greeting**

▨ **Counting**

▨ **Circle activities**

✳ SEND A SQUEEZE

See page 62.

✳ Put the children into pairs. They each tell their partner what they like to do when they are at the seaside. Allow several minutes for this and then ask the children to report their partner's preferred activity back to the circle.

✳ UNDER THE SEA
See page 52.

▪ Designated activity: PSHE

Remind the children about the 'character' who started a new school. Ask the children to think of ways in which a child who was new to their school might break the school rules. Look at examples, such as:

- Talking in lessons.
- Running in the school buildings.
- Damaging equipment.
- Talking to people impolitely.
- Calling children nasty names.
- Hurting other children.
- Taking someone else's property.

Ask the children to remind you why schools have rules.

▪ Free play

▪ Refreshments

▪ Wash up/story time

▪ Clapping rhyme/song/goodbye

T H U R S D A Y

The circle activities focus on participating, taking turns, speaking out, and watching and listening.

▪ Greeting

▪ Counting

▪ Circle activities

✳ THE BIG PICTURE
See page 25.

✳ The children complete the sentence stem 'In school, I like to _____', saying what their favourite activity in school is.

✳ An adult scribes each child's statement to add to the PSHE display.

✳ Play a game of categories using items in school. For example, anyone who likes counting, games, writing stories, drawing pictures or working on the computer.

▪ Designated activity: group game

✳ BOARD GAMES WITH ADULTS

▪ Free play

▪ Refreshments

▪ Wash up/story time

▪ Clapping rhyme/song/goodbye

W E E K 8

Monday	large die, beanbag, ingredients and utensils for cooking
Tuesday	small toy, expression cards, button and key, blindfold, paint, pencil crayons, A4 paper
Wednesday	photographs, ice hands, two bowls of water
Thursday	big picture, animal pictures, noisy object, blindfold, skittles and balls

M O N D A Y

The circle activities focus on participating, speaking out, and watching and listening.

▦ Greeting

▦ Counting

▦ Circle activities

✳ THE DIE GAME

See page 62.

✳ Explain to the children that they are going to think of areas where they might do better in school. Giving prompts, make a list of their ideas, for example, do more writing, try to make their work neater, try to learn a times table, finish a reading book, or play nicely at playtimes. Ask each child to complete the sentence stem 'This week in school, I will try to _____.' An adult scribes the children's statements to add to the PSHE display.

✳AFLOAT IN A BOAT

See page 23.

▦ Designated activity: cooking

✳ BUTTERFLY CAKES WITH CHOCOLATE SPREAD FILLING

Follow the recipe for small cakes (see page 57). When the cakes have cooled, scoop out a small circle from the top of each cake. Fill the indentation left in the cake with chocolate spread. Cut the cake pieces that you have scooped out into halves and press the halves into the chocolate filling on each cake to make butterfly wings.

▦ Free play

▦ Refreshments

▦ Wash up/story time

▦ Clapping rhyme/song/goodbye

TUESDAY

The circle activities focus on working cooperatively within a group, the children recognising emotion in themselves and others, expressing feelings appropriately, taking turns and speaking out.

▨ Greeting

▨ Counting

▨ Circle activities

✳ HUNT THE SMALL TOY
See page 58.

✳ Put the children into pairs. Place the expression cards face down on the floor and ask each pair to pick up one card. The children tell their partners what might make them feel like their expression card. The children show their card and report back to the circle their partner's statement.

✳BUTTON AND KEY
See page 21.

▨ Designated activity: art

The children paint the remaining half of the inside of their box to represent the sand. They paint the hull of their ship brown on both sides. On a piece of A4 paper, they can draw, colour and cut out items to put on to the background in their box, for example, shells, starfish and fish. Model the size they should draw their items to make sure they are not too large. When the paint is dry (this may be on another day) the children can glue their items on to the background. The sail is attached to the boat using a lollipop stick or a straw. The adults then hang the boat and shark from the top of the boxes to create a 3D picture.

▨ Free play

▨ Refreshments

▨ Wash up/story time

▨ Clapping rhyme/song/goodbye

WEDNESDAY

The circle activities focus on participating, watching and listening, speaking out, and the children recognising emotion in themselves and others.

▨ Greeting

▨ Counting

▨ Circle activities

✳ SEND A SMILE
See page 58.

✳ Choose a selection of photographs from the SEAL resources pack. Ask the children how each subject is feeling. Why might they be feeling like this? Finish with a happy expression and ask each child to complete the sentence stem 'I feel happy when _____.'

✳ IN THE DRIVING SEAT
See page 68.

▓ Designated activity: science

Prior to the lesson, create two 'ice hands' by filling surgical gloves with water, tying at the wrists and freezing. Remove the gloves gently (the fingers are quite fragile). Fill a bowl with water. Pass an ice hand round for the children to feel the weight. Ask if they think it will float or sink. As it feels quite heavy, the children generally think it will sink. Place the ice hand on the water and show the children that it floats – ice is less dense than water. Ask the children to guess how long it will take to melt. Write down their estimates. Place the other ice hand in a second bowl of water and put it outside. Ask the children to guess which ice hand will melt first and note down their answers.

Check the ice hands throughout the session. Talk to the children about ice forming on seas. Does it happen in our country? The salt in the sea prevents it from freezing until the temperature becomes very cold. Where does the sea become frozen?

▓ Free play

▓ Refreshments

▓ Wash up/story time

▓ Clapping rhyme/song/goodbye

T H U R S D A Y

The circle activities focus on participating, taking turns, speaking out, and watching and listening.

▓ Greeting

▓ Counting

▓ Circle activities

✳ THE BIG PICTURE
   See page 25.

✳ WHAT AM I? (YEAR 2+)
   See page 22.

✳ *WHO CAN THINK OF SOMETHING?*
   See page 52.

✳ DRAGON'S DEN
   See page 64.

▓ Designated activity: group game

✳ SKITTLES
   See page 60.

▓ Free play

▓ Refreshments

▓ Wash up/story time

▓ Clapping rhyme/song/goodbye

W E E K 9

Monday	everyday objects, ingredients and utensils for cooking
Tuesday	small toy, pirate hats (see page 129), black sugar paper, white paper circle, pencil crayons, glue sticks
Wednesday	N/A
Thursday	big picture, A4 paper, pencils, targets

M O N D A Y

The circle activities focus on working cooperatively within a group, speaking out, using expressive language, taking turns, and watching and listening.

■ **Greeting**

■ **Counting**

■ **Circle activities**

✳ ZOOM AND EEK
See page 55.

✳ MY OBJECT (YEAR 2+)
See page 22.

✳ *The children complete the sentences stem 'If I was an animal that lived in the sea, I would be a _____ because _____.'*

✳ UNDER THE SEA
See page 52.

■ **Designated activity: cooking**

✳ CHOCOLATE-CHIP COOKIES
See page 65.

■ **Free play**

■ **Refreshments**

■ **Wash up/story time**

■ **Clapping rhyme/song/goodbye**

T U E S D A Y

The circle activities focus on working cooperatively within a group, watching and listening, and participating.

■ **Greeting**

■ **Counting**

Circle activities

✳ HUNT THE SMALL TOY

See page 58.

✳ Say to the children, 'Well done for sitting nicely and listening well.' Ask the children what they need to do to listen well. Establish the following:

- Look at the person who is talking.
- Keep quiet.
- Sit still.
- Use their ears.
- Concentrate.

✳ FISH IN THE SEA

See page 59.

Designated activity: art

The children cut out their pirate hats from black sugar paper. They cut out a circle of white paper for the front, and draw and colour a pirate picture on to it. They stick the pirate picture on to the front of their hat. An adult measures the hat around their head and staples the two halves together.

Free play

Refreshments

Wash up/story time

Clapping rhyme/song/goodbye

WEDNESDAY

The circle activities focus on working cooperatively within a group, participating, speaking out, and watching and listening.

Greeting

Counting

Circle activities

✳ SEND A SMILE

See page 58.

✳ Ask the children what they could take to a pirate's party. The children offer suggestions that an adult writes on the board.

✳ WALKING A TIGHTROPE

See page 70.

Designated activity: PSHE

Prompt the children to offer suggestions of all the good things they like about school. Encourage them to think of things such as:

- learn how to read/write/count
- learn about their world

- learn how to get on with people
- enjoy games together
- eat together
- perform plays for their parents, or
- learn how to swim.

An adult scribes their statements to add to the PSHE display. Ask each child what they most enjoy learning.

■ **Free play**

■ **Refreshments**

■ **Wash up/story time**

■ **Clapping rhyme/song/goodbye**

T H U R S D A Y

The circle activities focus on working cooperatively within a group, taking turns, participating, speaking out, and watching and listening.

■ **Greeting**

■ **Counting**

■ **Circle activities**

✳ THE BIG PICTURE
See page 25.

✳ Put the children into groups of three or four. Ask them to work together to draw a person on a piece of A4 paper. Call them back to the circle and ask them how they did this task. Did they talk about it first? Did they take turns to draw? How did they work together? What do they need to do to work well together in a group? Who thinks they are good at working in a group?

✳ RABBIT'S EARS
See page 24.

■ **Designated activity: group game**

✳ TARGET PRACTICE
See page 63.

■ **Free play**

■ **Refreshments**

■ **Wash up/story time**

■ **Clapping rhyme/song/goodbye**

W E E K   1 0

Monday	photographs, button and key, blindfold, ingredients and utensils for cooking
Tuesday	small toy, large die, paper, paint
Wednesday	magician's cloak, cauldron, beanbag, magnets, metallic and non-metallic objects, card boats, paper clips, shallow tray of water
Thursday	big picture, items for 'giving instructions', parachute or items for team games

M O N D A Y

The circle activities focus on working cooperatively within a group, the children recognising emotion in themselves and others, and speaking out.

■ **Greeting**

■ **Counting**

■ **Circle activities**

✳ SEND A SMILE
   See page 58.

✳ Show the children a photograph of friends playing together from the SEAL resource pack. Ask the children how we know they are friends. How do their faces look? Ask the children what they like to do with their friends.

✳ BUTTON AND KEY
   See page 21.

■ **Designated activity: cooking**

✳ FRUITY BUNS
   See page 72.

■ **Free play**

■ **Refreshments**

■ **Wash up/story time**

■ **Clapping rhyme/song/goodbye**

TUESDAY

The circle activities focus on working cooperatively within a group, watching and listening, expressing feelings appropriately, speaking out, taking turns and forming positive relationships.

Greeting

Counting

Circle activities

✳ HUNT THE SMALL TOY

See page 58.

✳ SEND A SQUEEZE

See page 62.

✳ Commend the children for listening well. Ask them if they can remember the five things they need to do to listen well:

- Look at the person who is talking.
- Keep quiet.
- Sit still.
- Use their ears.
- Concentrate.

✳ Give one of the children a compliment, for example, 'I like the way you smile'. Explain that this is called a compliment – when you say something nice about somebody.

Tell the children that they are going to think of a compliment about the person sitting on their left. Go through some ideas with them beforehand. For example:

- I like the way you share toys
- I like the way you play with me
- I like the way you help tidy up
- I like the polite way you talk, or
- I like the way you make me laugh.

Each child and adult, in turn, gives a compliment to the person next to them. If anyone is stuck for ideas, the other children can offer suggestions for them to choose from.

✳ THE DIE GAME

See page 62.

Designated activity: art

The children paint their hands to make handprints. When these are dry, they or an adult cut around the hands and draw on eyes to make jellyfish. Add the jellyfish to the art display.

Free play

Refreshments

Wash up/story time

Clapping rhyme/song/goodbye

W E D N E S D A Y

The circle activities focus on working cooperatively within a group, forming positive relationships, speaking out and participating.

▦ **Greeting**

▦ **Counting**

▦ **Circle activities**

✳ ZOOM AND EEK

See page 55.

✳ MAGICIAN'S CLOAK

Make a spell for a good friend (see page 54). Ask the children what ingredients they would need to make a good friend, for example, kindness, sharing, fun, laughter, caring, taking turns or getting on.

✳ AFLOAT IN A BOAT

See page 23.

▦ **Designated activity: science**

Put the children into pairs. Let them play with magnets to discover how they attract and repel. Place a variety of magnetic and non-magnetic objects on to a tray and let the children see what objects are attracted to the magnet. Make two small boats from thick card and place a paper clip on each boat. Fill a shallow tray with water and float the card boats on the water. Let the children take turns to use their magnets underneath the tray to move the boats on the water.

▦ **Free play**

▦ **Refreshments**

▦ **Wash up/story time**

▦ **Clapping rhyme/song/goodbye**

T H U R S D A Y

The circle activities focus on participating, taking turns, speaking out and forming positive relationships.

▦ **Greeting**

▦ **Counting**

▦ **Circle activities**

✳ THE BIG PICTURE

See page 25.

✳ The children complete the sentence stem 'I am a good friend because _____.'

✳ Give them some ideas before the round. For example:

- I play nicely
- I share my toys
- I am kind
- I think of others, or
- I am helpful.

✳ GIVING INSTRUCTIONS
See page 20.

▨ **Designated activity: group game**

✳ PARACHUTE OR TEAM GAMES
See page 67.

▨ **Free play**

▨ **Refreshments**

▨ **Wash up/story time**

▨ **Clapping rhyme/song/goodbye**

W E E K   1 1

Monday	ingredients and utensils for cooking
Tuesday	small toy, animal pictures, noisy object, blindfold, parrots (see page 130), card, felt-tip pens, feathers, glue and stickers, 2p pieces, Blu-Tack
Wednesday	puppets or photograph
Thursday	big picture, button and key, blindfold

M O N D A Y

The circle activities focus on working cooperatively within a group, watching and listening, participating, speaking out and forming positive relationships.

▨ **Greeting**

▨ **Counting**

▨ **Circle activities**

✳ SEND A SQUEEZE
See page 62.

✳ Ask the children if they can remember what they need to do to listen well. Remind them of the five things they need to do (see page 86).

✳ Ask the children if they remember giving compliments. Model a few examples with the children. Ask the children how they feel when somebody pays them a compliment. Ask the children how they feel when someone is mean to them. How would they rather feel?

✳ Each child, in turn, pays a compliment to the child on their right.

✳ Ask the children to show you their happy faces, because someone has paid them a compliment.

✳ FISH IN THE SEA
See page 59.

▦ Designated activity: cooking

✳ RICE KRISPIES CAKES

Use two slabs of chocolate. Although this recipe involves the use of hot water, we have never yet, during eight years of making these cakes, had an accident. However, if you decide that you do not want the children to be in close contact with hot water, one of the adults could melt the chocolate during the circle activities.

Place a bowl into a pan of hot water for each group. You could limit the activity to two groups, with an adult holding the pan, or designate an older, sensible child to perform this role in each group. The children are each given part of a slab of chocolate. They break the chocolate into chunks, which they place into the bowl. The children take turns to stir the chocolate until it has melted. They then take turns to stir Rice Krispies into the melted chocolate. They then spoon the mixture into paper cake cases and these are placed into the fridge to cool. If the children have made a sufficient amount, they can each take a cake home.

▦ Free play

▦ Refreshments

▦ Wash up/story time

▦ Clapping rhyme/song/goodbye

T U E S D A Y

The circle activities focus on working cooperatively within a group, participating, taking turns, speaking out, and watching and listening.

▦ Greeting

▦ Counting

▦ Circle activities

✳ HUNT THE SMALL TOY
See page 58.

✳ WHAT AM I? (YEAR 2+)
See page 22.

✳ *WHO CAN THINK OF SOMETHING?*
See page 52.

✳ DRAGON'S DEN
See page 64.

▦ Designated activity: art

✳ PARROTS

The children cut a parrot out of card. They colour the parrot with bright felt-tip pens. They can glue coloured feathers on to the tails. Give each child a 2p piece and a small piece of Blu-Tack. Tell them that if they put the 2p piece in the correct place on their parrot, it will balance on the edge of the table (see the diagram on page 130). If the children cannot work this out by themselves, show them what to do. Add the parrots to your art display.

■ **Free play**

■ **Refreshments**

■ **Wash up/story time**

■ **Clapping rhyme/song/goodbye**

W E D N E S D A Y

The circle activities focus on participating, watching and listening, and taking turns.

■ **Greeting**

■ **Counting**

■ **Circle activities**

⁕ SEND A SMILE
   See page 58.

⁕ RABBIT'S EARS
   See page 24.

⁕ UNDER THE SEA
   See page 52.

■ **Designated activity: PSHE**

Describe a situation in which two friends fall out. Use puppets or a suitable photograph from the SEAL resource pack to act out a scene.

   • Ask the children how the friends are feeling.
   • Who can show a face to express this feeling?
   • What could the children do if they fall out with a friend to make the situation better?
   • Ask for volunteers to role play 'making up'.

⁕ The children complete the sentence stem 'It's not good to fall out with friends because
   _____.'

■ **Free play**

■ **Refreshments**

■ **Wash up/story time**

■ **Clapping rhyme/song/goodbye**

T H U R S D A Y

The circle activities focus on watching and listening, participating and speaking out.

■ **Greeting**

■ **Counting**

■ **Circle activities**

⁕ THE BIG PICTURE
   See page 25.

✳ WHAT COULD I TAKE ON A PIRATE SHIP FOR A LONG JOURNEY?
See page 23.

✳ BUTTON AND KEY
See page 21.

▨ Designated activity: drama

Make sure that the children have plenty of space to move around. They are going to do some acting about 'under the sea'. Tell them that they are going to pretend they are seaweed, floating in the current of the sea. They can wave their arms and move their bodies, but they must stand still.

• Put them into pairs and explain that they are going to pretend to be crabs. One child stands behind the other and grasps the waist of the child in front. They can only move sideways.

• Put them into groups of three. They are now going to pretend to be jellyfish. The children stand facing one another and place their arms around each other's shoulders. They must try to move together.

• Now the children are going to pretend to be sharks. They put their arms out in front of them as the shark's jaws, opening and closing the shark's big mouth. Warn the children not to attack each other.

• Place a selection of obstacles around the room. Ask the children to stand in a long line, one behind the other. They grasp the waist of the child in front. They are going to pretend they are a long sea serpent. The child in front leads the sea serpent slowly around the obstacles. Every so often, ask the child in front to join the back of the line so that each child has a chance to lead the sea serpent.

• Ask the children to form a 'shoal' of little fish. Can they all move together?

• End the session with the children being a sea creature of their choice. They must swim around, avoiding all the other sea creatures.

▨ Free play

▨ Refreshments

▨ Wash up/story time

▨ Clapping rhyme/song/goodbye

W E E K   1 2

Monday	beanbag, ingredients and utensils for cooking
Tuesday	small toy, everyday objects, magician's cloak, cauldron, items for 'giving instructions', Christmas card
Wednesday	photograph, large die, 2 litre bottle of water, jellyfish (see page 126)
Thursday	big picture, noisy object, blindfold, pirate games, party food

M O N D A Y

The circle activities focus on working cooperatively within a group, participating, speaking out, watching and listening, and taking turns.

Devising a suitable programme

■ **Greeting**

■ **Counting**

■ **Circle activities**

✳ ZOOM AND EEK

See page 55.

✳ The children complete the sentence stem 'The present I would most like for Christmas is
_____.'

✳AFLOAT IN A BOAT

See page 23.

■ **Designated activity: cooking**

✳ SMALL CAKES

See page 57 for the recipe for these cakes. Put all the sponge mixture into a large square tin and bake. When the cake is cool, cut it into squares and then half the squares to make triangles. Make up some green icing. The children decorate their cakes with green icing and silver balls, or sprinkles, to make Christmas trees.

■ **Free play**

■ **Refreshments**

■ **Wash up/story time**

■ **Clapping rhyme/song/goodbye**

TUESDAY

The circle activities focus on working cooperatively within a group, speaking out, using expressive language, watching and listening, participating.

■ **Greeting**

■ **Counting**

■ **Circle activities**

✳ HUNT THE SMALL TOY

See page 58.

✳ MY OBJECT (YEAR 2+)

See page 22.

✳ MAGICIAN'S CLOAK

Make a happy Christmas spell (see page 54).

✳ CATEGORIES

See page 57.

✳ GIVING INSTRUCTIONS

See page 20.

▧ Designated activity: art

The children can make a Christmas card of your choice if this is appropriate at your school. Otherwise, they could make an additional item for the art display, such as finger painting small fish to create a shoal.

▧ Free play

▧ Refreshments

▧ Wash up/story time

▧ Clapping rhyme/song/goodbye

W E D N E S D A Y

The circle activities focus on working cooperatively within a group, the children recognising emotion in themselves and others, expressing feelings appropriately, participating and taking turns.

▧ Greeting

▧ Counting

▧ Circle activities

✳ SEND A SMILE

See page 58.

✳ Using a photograph from the SEAL resource pack, show a child with an angry face. Ask the children how the child is feeling. Why might the child be feeling this way? Ask the children to show you angry faces. What makes them angry? How do their bodies feel when they are angry? What can they do to make themselves feel better? Ask everyone to show you a happy face.

✳ THE DIE GAME

See page 62.

▧ Designated activity: science

✳ A DIVING JELLYFISH

Make a jellyfish (see page 126) so that it only just floats. Put the jellyfish into a 2 litre plastic bottle filled with water. Squeeze the sides of the bottle to make the jellyfish dive. Release the sides and the jellyfish floats back up to the surface. Let the children all have a turn to make the jellyfish dive.

Ask the children what helps them to stay afloat when they go swimming – armbands. Ask them what is in the armbands – air. The air in the straw keeps the jellyfish afloat. When the bottle is squeezed, the air is forced out of the straw by the water and the jellyfish sinks.

▧ Free play

▧ Refreshments

▧ Wash up/story time

▧ Clapping rhyme/song/goodbye

T H U R S D A Y

The circle activities focus on watching and listening, participating and speaking out.

■ **Greeting**

■ **Counting**

■ **Circle activities**

＊ THE BIG PICTURE
   See page 25.

＊ DRAGON'S DEN
   See page 64.

＊ WHO CAN THINK OF SOMETHING?
   See page 52.

■ **Designated activity: pirate party**

Think of some suitable pirate games for the children to play. Some examples are given below.

＊ MUSICAL ISLANDS
   Make a drawing of a pirate on a large sheet of paper. Cut out a pirate's hat (see page 129). The children take turns to wear a blindfold and put the hat on the pirate.

＊ TREASURE, TREASURE, PIRATE
   Play this game just like 'Duck, duck, goose'.

＊ MUSICAL PIRATE STATUES

＊ MUSICAL COINS
   Place coins on a table that the children walk around. When the music stops, the children pick up a coin. Remove a coin each time until there is a winner.

＊ BLIND PIRATE'S BLUFF
   The children stand in a circle. Choose one child to wear a blindfold and ask them to stand in the centre of the circle. Turn the child around several times. They then walk forward with arms outstretched until they touch a child in the circle. They ask, 'Who is this pirate I've captured?' The captured child must disguise their voice and answer giving a pirate name (for example: 'It's cut-throat Sam' or 'It's peg-leg Jake'). The child wearing the blindfold must try to guess the identity of their captive.

＊ Arrange the party food that you have brought in on the table. Ask the children to think of suitably horrid pirate names for each dish, for example, cocktail sausages could be dead pirates' fingers and crisps could be crusty skin flakes. The children put on their pirate hats and sit at the table to eat their party food.

W E E K   1 3

You will hopefully have this week to prepare for the next term. Remember to inform the teachers and parents that your group is finishing and will not operate during the last week.

CHAPTER 13

Working with the parents

I consider this a very important aspect of our roles, as so much can be achieved by developing a positive relationship with a child's parents. I have found that many of the parents of our children, mothers usually, as they are the ones who generally provide the care during the day, feel marginalised from other parents and staff at the school.

They may, themselves, lack relationship skills and have low academic ability, or social problems. They may feel inferior and unable to deal with the comments from teachers about their child. They may also be defensive, believing that members of staff do not understand or like their child. Quite often these parents deal with such problems by avoiding both consultation evenings and social events at the school.

Sadly, there are other parents and members of staff who lack empathy and are intolerant of these individuals. They do not stop to consider the difficulties in their lives and prefer to blame rather than offer understanding and assistance. I am amazed that capable and intelligent people can, in spite of their knowledge and training, be so condemnatory of others. It is, perhaps, the easy option.

Try to adopt the same attitude with the parents that you have with the children. Show them that not only do you like and care for their children, you also like and care about them. Whenever possible, make time for a brief and friendly chat when you encounter them in the playground, and try to remember to look pleased to see them.

Emphasise their children's strengths and highlight where improvements are being made. It is important to adopt a positive tone, as negative thinking about a child's behaviour indicates that you do not expect change to occur. This attitude may well prolong the behaviour you want to discourage.

Parents, who are generally absent from other school functions, regularly attend the tea and biscuit sessions we hold each term. I have found this to be a very effective approach. Not only do the children make invitations for these events, but I also speak to each parent individually, expressing my hope that they will attend.

Most parents already hold a less negative view of the group than the mainstream school because of the feedback from their children. Knowing that their children enjoy being with us and are making good progress encourages them to see the group in a positive and more hopeful light. It may be the first time since their child started school that they are hearing positive reports of success.

It is a good idea to hold regular drop-in sessions after school one day each week and make sure that you listen to any concerns the parents might voice, attentively and with genuine empathy. The majority of parents do their very best for their children and just because the children do not meet the standards we deem acceptable, we should not dismiss their efforts.

It is also worthwhile to canvass the parents' views each year by asking them to complete a short questionnaire (see page 122). Make sure to take note of their comments and make any improvements to your practice where necessary.

Occasionally a tricky situation may develop where a parent takes issue with the way in which a child's class teacher treats a child as opposed to how the adults within the group behave. The parent may perceive the class teacher as being less tolerant and sympathetic towards their child.

Care must be taken not to alienate the class teacher or escalate the issue. It is generally sufficient to explain to the parent that the child may behave in a more positive way within the group, but the provision specifically caters for fewer children in order to meet their needs more appropriately and successfully.

You can reassure the parent that, as the child develops a more positive attitude within the classroom as well, the teacher will be able to respond likewise.

CHAPTER 14

Working with outside agencies

As the group is part-time, referrals of children to outside agencies takes place via the class teacher, in consultation with the Special Educational Needs Coordinator (SENCO) and the head teacher. The procedure will, of course, vary from school to school.

We supply information for meetings about the children, detailing their behaviour within the group. This may be in the form of a written statement or by attending a meeting in person.

Sometimes, an educational psychologist or behaviour support adviser will visit to observe a child, especially where the child's behaviour is very different to within their mainstream class.

We have also had many visits from interested parties, wanting to observe our group in practice. Numerous teachers and LSAs have come to gain information, as they want to set up a similar provision in their own schools. Other professional workers in education or social services are interested in seeing what the provision offers and how the intervention works successfully.

In the interests of promoting the intervention, we have always been very pleased to welcome visitors.

CHAPTER 15

Appointing the staff

This may seem an unnecessary inclusion in the book, but in my experience it is vital to appoint the correct staff if you want to ensure that the intervention is successful.

It probably goes without saying that the staff should be experienced, but they also need to possess the following knowledge and qualities:

- A basic understanding of the underlying causes of the children's behaviour.
- A basic knowledge of the causes of sound/poor self-esteem.
- A basic understanding of the developmental stages that young children go through.
- An understanding of the need to create a warm, familiar and safe environment for the children.
- An understanding of the need to provide set routines for the children.
- A non-judgemental attitude towards the children's background and family.
- The ability to 'bounce back' after any setbacks.
- An optimistic approach to effecting change in the children.
- A belief in the goals of the intervention.
- Unlimited patience, dedication and a sense of humour.

At least one of the members of staff needs to have a proven record of good discipline. This is really important in dealing with the more challenging children in the group and creating a safe environment for all group members.

It has been our experience over the years that we often need to go beyond the requirements and duties stated in our contracts and we have frequently given our own time, in producing resources, for example, to ensure the quality of the intervention. For this reason, you need to try to appoint staff who are willing to give more than they are asked when the occasion demands.

It is also important to delegate a third named member of staff to act as a stand-in, in case one of the adults is away. Your head teacher may need to negotiate this with a sympathetic member of staff if it involves them losing their TA for an afternoon.

CHAPTER 16

Final thoughts

Providing a modified curriculum for the children who were failing to access the National Curriculum has proved to be a very successful intervention in our school. However, as with any strategy, the quality of delivery has to be maintained if its effectiveness is to continue. It is very easy for standards to begin to slip after the initial enthusiasm and drive have worn off.

If you notice that you are becoming lax in your procedures, or your approach to the children is becoming less positive, you may need to give yourselves a pep talk to remind yourselves that the success of the group depends on good practice and a positive attitude.

Canvassing both the teaching staff and the parents for their views in an anonymous ballot will help to keep you on your toes. You need to make sure that you act on valid criticism to promote better practice. Also, review the progress made by the children each year to ensure that they continue to improve.

Having the modified curriculum group has brought great benefits to the individual children who attend, and also to the whole school community. It enhances the provision for those children with additional social and emotional needs and demonstrates that there is a place for everybody within the school environment, where all children can enjoy success and be valued. Teachers have become more skilled at assessing their pupils' needs, with a more empathetic approach to children who are failing to learn and an understanding that challenging or withdrawn behaviours are responses to difficult situations. Members of staff have learned that these behaviours can be changed with a suitable intervention and that children do not have to be stuck with these behaviours. This knowledge enables everyone to be more patient, helpful and hopeful with troubled children.

It has been a gratifying experience to work with the children and witness the transformation in their ability to cope in their mainstream classrooms, and the transformation in their perception of school as a whole. Showing the children that they have skills and competencies, that they are liked and valued and that they are not 'failures' has provided them with a more positive self-image. This, in turn, enables them to function more successfully and to cope with the demands made upon them in their classes.

I believe that every school should provide a modified curriculum to meet the needs of struggling children. The curriculum needs to move away from its current, narrow perspective and provide a broader approach to education. There needs to be a real attempt to fulfil the criteria in the 'Every Child Matters' document rather than the current over-emphasis on academic achievement and to provide a curriculum that will help all children enjoy success in school and move towards a useful and fulfilled future (see www.everychildmatters.gov.uk).

What teachers say

- He is much more able to work with other children without the need for constant facilitation.
- I see him smile now and he always remembers when it is a Sunflower day.
- He is now beginning to learn how other children get on with each other and is starting to talk about his friends.
- She is much happier now and calmer in class.
- He joins in now with greater confidence in our class activities.
- Now she is proud of the work she does; before she did not used to care about it.
- To begin with, his mum was really worried about him coming to Sunflowers, but now she thinks it has done him lots of good.
- She has learned to be more caring of the children around her and has even shown concern about children who are looking worried, passing on her concern to the teacher.
- Children come back from Sunflowers and talk to the class about what they have done, where before, even finding the confidence to stand up in front of the class was lacking.

CHAPTER 17

Resources

Vision statement

Before you embark on your policy document, it is a good idea to produce a vision statement of what you are hoping to achieve. An example is given below:

- A successful intervention strategy that will enable children to remain in mainstream education.
- An intervention that is not driven by academic targets.
- An intervention that has clear success criteria that is quantifiable.
- An intervention that provides a safe place for children where they are accepted and supported.
- An intervention that recognises the varying needs of the children and makes suitable provision to address those needs.
- An intervention that creates happier children who enjoy a positive experience of school.
- An intervention that is a valuable use of resources.
- An intervention that is seen as successful and essential by both the whole school community and the parents.
- An intervention that specifically helps children in danger of exclusion.

Policy document

Introduction

- Our group provides a modified curriculum to a maximum of twelve children in a nurturing environment.
- The group is an intervention for those children who are unable to access learning successfully in their mainstream classroom. This may be due to learning difficulties, emotional or behavioural difficulties, or disorders on the autistic spectrum.
- Our group meets on four afternoons a week, with the children spending the mornings and all day Friday in their mainstream classes.
- The group caters for children from Reception to Year 4.

- Two experienced staff run the group. In the absence of either team member, a designated member of staff takes their place.

Our aims

- To provide a small-scale setting in which children are provided with a modified curriculum more suited to their needs.
- To have a predictable, calm and purposeful environment and timetable, free from curriculum pressures.
- To enhance the learning and social skills of the children, raise their self-esteem and help them towards a more positive identity, enabling their successful reintegration.
- To develop positive relationships between adults and children, building trust, confidence and reliability.
- To develop responsibility for oneself and others.
- To help children learn appropriate behaviour.
- To help children learn to make decisions and wise choices through understanding the consequences of certain ways of behaving.
- To work in partnership with teachers and parents to achieve a consistency of approach at home and school.
- To provide ongoing assessment.
- To prevent possible exclusion.

Inclusive practice

In the group, we recognise that every child matters and aim to respond to each child's needs by taking into account their:

- Cultural background
- Life experiences
- Strengths
- Communication needs
- Emotional and social needs
- Developmental needs
- Physical needs.

Setting

- The modified curriculum group is a self-contained setting with toilet and kitchen facilities.
- The room has a homely atmosphere.
- The room provides space for a formal work area, play areas and a quiet area.
- A small adjoining room provides a separate area for children to sit alone and reflect on their behaviour.

The role of the adult workers

- The role of the adult is to sustain nurturing relationships with the children who attend.

- The adults should be good role models, demonstrating appropriate and positive behaviour that is consistent and continuous.
- The adults should recognise that children perceive themselves as worthwhile through positive and affirming relationships.

The curriculum

- The group provides a modified curriculum that is suited to the children's needs.
- Literacy and numeracy are covered in the children's mainstream classes.
- The group provides a modified curriculum in art, science, drama, PE and PSHE. Cooking and gardening are also included.
- There is a daily focus on learning and social skills.
- The group sessions are divided into small, manageable chunks of time, with each activity serving a clear purpose.
- Each session offers the security of a familiar and consistent structure as follows:
  - greeting ritual
  - circle time activities
  - designated activity of the day
  - free play
  - tidying away equipment and laying the table
  - refreshments
  - washing up and story time
  - clapping rhyme or song
  - ending ritual.
- The circle time activities focus on the following valuable skills:
  - taking turns
  - watching and listening
  - learning from others
  - speaking out in front of others
  - using expressive language
  - following instructions
  - trying something new
  - developing a positive attitude to participation
  - forming positive relationships
  - using agreed codes of behaviour
  - initiating activities with other children
  - learning to respond to sanctions
  - considering the rights and needs of themselves and others.
- Activities are weighted towards the children's PSHE development.
- Activities are designed to offer children criteria for doing well that guarantees success. The aim is to boost a child's self-esteem and give them a sense that they can be competent and capable.

Assessment

- The children are assessed twice a year using a Boxall Profile and a Goodman's Strengths and Difficulties Questionnaire.

- A written assessment is provided at a child's annual review if required.
- Assessment findings are discussed with each child's teacher, the SENCO and the head teacher.

Referral

The following types of children are considered for inclusion in the group:

- Children who appear to be emotionally insecure, which could present itself as a lack of self-acceptance, low self-worth or a lack of trust.
- Children who are withdrawn and unresponsive.
- Children with poor social skills who are demanding or uncooperative, or who cannot share.
- Children with a poor attention span.
- Children who demonstrate immature behaviour.
- Children who behave aggressively, impulsively or inappropriately in other ways.
- Children who find change upsetting.
- Children who appear unable to integrate into a mainstream classroom.

Referral procedure

- When a vacancy arises in the group, class teachers are invited to put forward children who they consider will benefit from attending the group.
- These children are assessed using Goodman's Strengths and Difficulties Questionnaire and, if this achieves an abnormal score, the teacher then completes a Boxall Profile on that child.
- If a decision is made to invite a child to join the group, a letter is sent home to inform the parents/carers and they are invited in for a consultation with the head teacher.
- The parents visit the group setting to be shown around and to look at the timetable in operation within the group.
- The parents are given a booklet to share with their child, prior to them joining the group.

Partnership with parents and carers

- We recognise the importance of involving parents/carers of a child in the process of their education.
- Each parent receives a copy of our leaflet explaining the group and detailing who we are and what we do.
- Parents are kept informed of their child's progress through informal weekly chats and written reports, twice yearly.
- Our aim is to develop positive relationships with the parents and offer support and advice when appropriate.
- Parents are invited to join the group for part of a session at the end of each term to enjoy refreshments with the children and to view their work.

Reintegration

- The children's reintegration to mainstream classes is determined from the results of their Boxall Profiles, assessment by the group's staff and discussion with their class teachers.

- The period of reintegration is generally carried out over a period of half a term, during which time the children's responses and progress are monitored closely.

- The children begin the process of reintegration by remaining for one or two afternoons in their mainstream classes.

- The class teachers encourage the children to talk in a class circle time about their experiences in the group.

- The child completes a reintegration sheet with an adult from the group.

Success criteria

We shall be successful if:

- We provide positive, affirming and manageable sessions.
- Time to reflect on inappropriate behaviour is seen as an effective consequence.
- Incentives that are offered are seen as desirable by the children.
- What is acceptable and unacceptable behaviour is made clear.
- Any inappropriate behaviour is spotted quickly and dealt with effectively.
- The routines within the group provide security.
- The activities are tailored to guarantee success.
- The children are given unconditional warmth and acceptance.
- There is a focus on group building activities.
- The children receive greater attention.
- The children can gain a more positive identity than the one they have learned elsewhere.
- The children gain confidence and are more willing to participate and take on new challenges.
- The sense of success enables the children to put more effort into their work.
- There is plenty of humour and fun.
- The children see school as a positive experience and enjoy attending.
- The children are successfully reintegrated into their mainstream classes.

Useful resources

For further information about:

- providing a modified curriculum and details of INSET courses: Helen Sonnet at helen@positiveteaching.co.uk
- Stern Structural Arithmetic: enquiries@mathsextra.com
- Goodman's Strengths and Difficulties Questionnaire: www.sdqinfo.com
- the Boxall Profile: www.nurturegroups.org
- the Primary Review: www.primaryreview.org.uk
- 'Every Child Matters': www.everychildmatters.gov.uk

Useful publications

Mosley, J. and Sonnet, H. (2002) *101 Games for Self-Esteem*, Cambridge: LDA.

—— and —— (2002) *Making Waves (parachute games)*, Cambridge: LDA.

—— and —— (2003) *101 Games for Social Skills*, Cambridge: LDA.

—— and —— (2005) *Clapping Games*, Trowbridge: Positive Press.

—— and —— (2005) *Singing Games*, Trowbridge: Positive Press.

—— and —— (2006) *Helping Children Deal with Anger*, Cambridge: LDA.

Photocopiable resources

Example of a welcoming booklet

Hayesdown First School

Sunflower Group

WELCOME TO SUNFLOWER GROUP

We aim to:

* Provide a happy and secure environment for learning
* Provide a timetable that is stimulating and enjoyable
* Ensure that all children feel welcome and valued
* Encourage every child to have a positive self-image
* Encourage respect for other people and property
* Reinforce the school's ethos and Golden Rules

1

Do art   Do cooking
Do science   Do drama
Do gardening Do P.E.

Play group games such as parachute games and skittles
Play circle games
Play board games

HAVE FUN!

We look forward to welcoming your child into Sunflowers

6

Example of a welcoming booklet *continued*

SUNFLOWER GROUP

Sunflower group provides a homely and welcoming atmosphere.

The group caters for up to twelve children with two adults to supervise and support them.

We are committed to encouraging the children's individual development.

Each child has targets throughout the year which we help them to achieve.

In addition to the work area, there is a space for play and a quiet area. We also have a small side room, where children can sit and reflect on their behaviour or spend a little time on their own or with an adult.

3

When your child is ready, they will begin the reintegration process back to their mainstream class, beginning with one or two afternoons a week.

You are welcome to visit us and find out about your child's progress.

Come and share any worries or concerns you may have about your child with us. We are available every Thursday after school.

We hope that your child will enjoy being part of Sunflower Group.

4

In Sunflowers we:

Learn to share
Talk about feelings
Have our own targets
Make good friends

Learn new activities
Learn songs and clapping rhymes
Learn to listen and talk to each other
Learn to work and play with different people

5

HOW WE WORK

In the afternoon, after registration, your child will be collected from their class by a member of Sunflower's staff. They will remain with us all afternoon until home-time, so on the days that your child attends, you will need to collect them from Sunflowers.

2

Positive Intervention for Pupils who Struggle at School, Routledge © Helen Sonnet 2010

Example of a reintegration form

Name:

_____

This is a picture of me
in Sunflowers

In Sunflowers we:

• Cook

• Garden

• Do science

• Play games

• Make things

and join in lots of
activities

My favourite thing in
Sunflowers is

I am in

_____

class

Soon I will be
spending afternoons
with my class.

My teacher will be
pleased if I:

• _____

• _____

• _____

Positive Intervention for Pupils who Struggle at School, Routledge © Helen Sonnet 2010

Example of a weekly timetable

Monday	Tuesday	Wednesday	Thursday	Comments
Greeting	Greeting	Greeting	Greeting	
Remind children of rules	Ask children to tell you why we have our rules	Round: 'One kind thing I did this week was _ _ _ _ _ _ _'	Show children photos of people with different expressions	*Flowerpots, seeds and compost for Monday*
Circle activities:	Circle activities:		• How do they feel?	
Softball challenge: 'One interesting thing I did at the weekend was _ _ _ _ _ _ _'	Farmyard Expressions: ask children to hold up the correct face for a variety of situations	Circle activities: What am I? Look at the dragon.	• What could make you feel like this? Circle activities:	*Faces from the SEAL resources pack; and clay for Tuesday*
Afloat in a boat.		Tactile activities: • play dough	Button and key	*Make play dough and prepare paint trays for Wednesday*
Gardening: plant sunflower seeds in pots.	Art: make clay garden animals	• sand • sticking • finger painting	Who can think of something?	
Draw and decorate name label for pot.	Free play	Free play	Group activity: parachute games	*Photos from SEAL resources pack, parachute and games book for Thursday*
Free play	Drink and biscuit	Drink and biscuit	Free play	
Drink and biscuit	Wash up/story time	Wash up/story time	Drink and biscuit	
Wash up/story time	Goodbye	Goodbye	Goodbye	
Goodbye				

Example of an information letter sent to all parents

SUNFLOWER GROUP

Sunflower group was set up to offer a more suitable curriculum to children who are experiencing difficulties accessing the curriculum in their classes. With a modified timetable, Sunflowers can help the children in the following ways:

- to develop the building blocks for the key learning skills
- to develop a positive disposition to participate
- to form positive relationships with adults and other children
- to use agreed codes of behaviour
- to initiate activities with other children
- to learn to respond to restraints.

Sunflower group offers places to children through referral by their class teacher, followed by an assessment using a Boxall Profile, a diagnostic set of prepared response items, that highlights the areas of concern.

The Boxall Profile is subsequently administered at regular intervals to assess the children's progress and their eligibility for reintegration into afternoon classes.

The timetable is carefully planned to offer the children frequent opportunities for developing the key learning skills of looking, listening, speaking, thinking and concentrating. In addition, there is a focus on enhancing short-term memory skills and promoting a positive self-image.

The majority of children who have attended Sunflower group have shown a significant improvement in the classroom.

_____

Positive Intervention for Pupils who Struggle at School, Routledge © Helen Sonnet 2010

Example of an information letter sent to all parents
continued

SUNFLOWER GROUP

Some myths about Sunflower Group

"Only naughty children attend"

Not true. Although a few children may show challenging behaviour in the classroom, the majority attend Sunflower group for other reasons. Moreover, with a timetable suited to their needs, children are less likely to behave inappropriately.

"The children just play all afternoon"

Not true. There is a slot of around twenty minutes for independent play, during which the adults can observe the children's social interactions.

The remainder of the afternoon is highly structured and the children achieve a considerable amount of work.

"The children will fall even further behind with their work"

Not true. Remember, the children have been referred because they are not currently accessing the curriculum successfully. They still have the core subjects of literacy and numeracy in morning classes and the structured activities in Sunflower group focus on developing key learning skills. The evidence so far shows an improvement, rather than a deterioration, in their achievements in the classroom.

"The children will pick up bad habits in the group"

Not true. Behavioural boundaries are consistent and well-controlled. With fewer children and a very structured timetable, there is less incidence of bad behaviour. The children are kept occupied with suitable, interesting activities, which is the best deterrent to inappropriate behaviour. Moreover, there is a particular focus on positive behaviour within the group.

We hope this letter will give you a better understanding of the aims and purpose of Sunflower group.

_____

Positive Intervention for Pupils who Struggle at School, Routledge © Helen Sonnet 2010

The story of the mouse family

THE MOUSE FAMILY

CAST

Storyteller (an adult)

The giant (an adult)

The mouse family

SETTING THE SCENE

If it is a warm day, you can act out the play outdoors. If you are able, drape a curtain or large piece of material over something in one corner of the room to create a 'mouse hole'. It must allow the children to stand up and move around underneath. In the mouse hole, you will need a picnic basket, plastic plates and cups, and a picnic blanket. Place items of plastic food around the setting for the mouse children to collect.

There was once a family of mice who lived in a warm, comfortable hole under a tree trunk. There was a mother mouse, a father mouse and lots of mice children. (*The children group together as for a family portrait.*)

One sunny day, mother mouse decides it would be fun to have a picnic. She calls all of the mouse children to her and tells them each to collect something to eat for the picnic. (*The mouse children scurry off to look around the room for the plastic food. The mother then packs the food items into the picnic basket, while the father collects the plates and cups and puts them into a bag.*)

At last, everything is ready and the family set off with their basket, bags and rug. Father mouse thinks it would be a good idea to have their picnic in a cool, shady wood and he leads the way along the path, calling all the mouse children to follow and not get left behind. (*Father mouse leads mother mouse and the mouse children along a path, if outside, or an imaginary path in the room. He can call to the children, 'keep up' and 'don't get left behind'.*)

When the family reach the woods, mother and father mouse spread out the blanket and set out the picnic. Everyone sits on the blanket to enjoy their food and drink. (*The children mime handing out plates, food and cups and pretend to eat and drink.*)

When the family have finished their picnic, mother mouse tells the mouse children that they can go into the woods and play for a while. However, she warns them not to go too far, as she does not want anyone to get lost. Mother and father mouse tidy away

The story of the mouse family *continued*

THE MOUSE FAMILY

the picnic items, then, feeling a little sleepy, they settle down for a short nap. (*Father and mother mouse mime the actions described while the mouse children move away and pretend to play with each other. Two children are chosen to go some distance from the rest and sit on the floor next to the adult who is playing the friendly giant.*)

After a while, mother and father mouse wake up. It is beginning to get a little chilly so they call the mouse children, telling them it is time to go home. The mouse children come scurrying up, but when they do a head count the mouse parents realise that two of the children are missing. No one knows where they are. (*The children act out the actions described.*)

The worried mouse parents decide they must set off together to look for the missing mouse children. Father mouse leads his family through the woods, climbing over boulders and crawling through tunnels of brambles, until they arrive at a huge house surrounded by tall trees. Luckily, the door is ajar, so the mouse family slip into the hall and tiptoe to the kitchen. (*The children mime the actions described, using the natural terrain, if outside, or by using an obstacle that has been set up prior to the acting to climb over and crawl through. When they reach the giant's house, they tiptoe quietly into the kitchen.*)

A very strange sight greets them. A large and terrifying giant is seated on a chair by a table. The missing mouse children are next to the giant. The mouse family are very frightened as they think that the giant is going to eat the two little mice. However, they see that the giant is feeding the mouse children tiny scraps of food and patting them gently on their heads. (*The giant and mice mime the actions described.*)

The giant does not look fierce at all. He is a smiling, friendly-looking giant, so father mouse decides to approach him. When father mouse asks the giant why he has taken his two mouse children, the giant looks sad. He tells father mouse that he is lonely. He was not going to hurt the little mice; he just wanted them to be his pets and keep him company. (*The children and adult act out the actions described.*)

Father mouse tells the giant that he cannot keep the mouse children as pets, but the family will come to visit him every week. The giant and the mouse family join hands and stand in a circle as they sing a song together. (*The children and adult sing a song such as 'If you're happy and you know it'.*)

Positive Intervention for Pupils who Struggle at School, Routledge © Helen Sonnet 2010

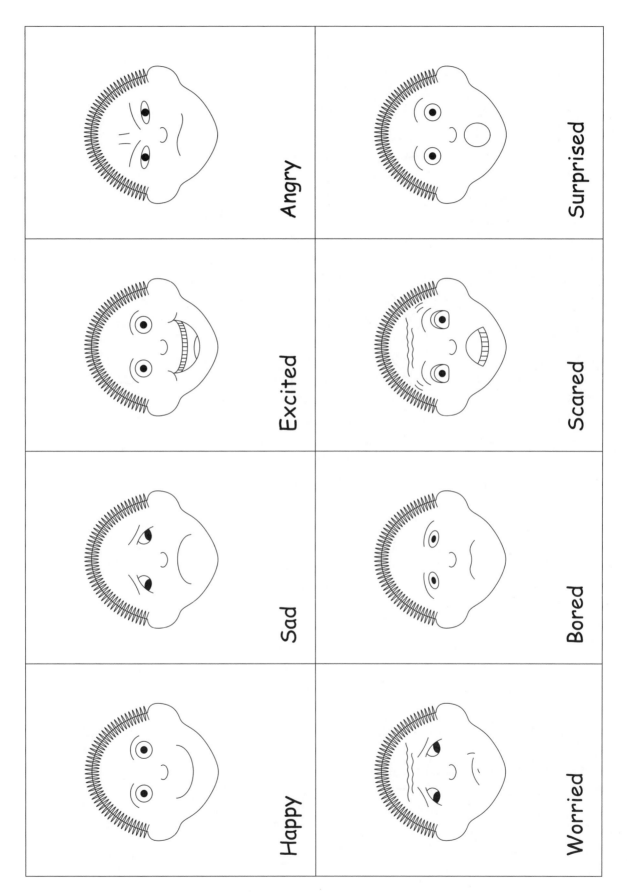

Angry

Surprised

Excited

Scared

Sad

Bored

Happy

Worried

Positive Intervention for Pupils who Struggle at School, Routledge © Helen Sonnet 2010

Place on fold

Enlarge onto A3 paper or card

Class display

Positive Intervention for Pupils who Struggle at School, Routledge © Helen Sonnet 2010

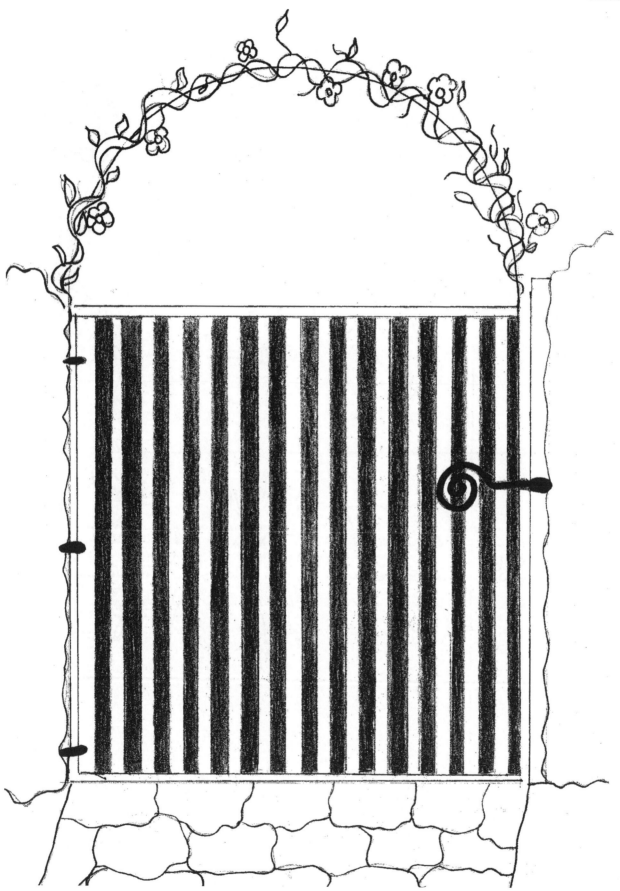

Positive Intervention for Pupils who Struggle at School, Routledge © Helen Sonnet 2010

Sunflowers

Dear parents, we would be very grateful if you could take a few minutes to fill in this questionnaire. If you have any further comments to add please use the space at the bottom of the page.

Thank you,

	Disagree				Agree	
I feel that my child has benefited from their time in Sunflowers	0	1	2	3	4	5
I have been given enough information about Sunflowers	0	1	2	3	4	5
I have been kept up to date with my child's progress	0	1	2	3	4	5
I feel that Sunflowers has had a positive effect on my child at home	0	1	2	3	4	5
I feel that Sunflowers has had a positive effect on my child at school	0	1	2	3	4	5
I think that my child gets on better in their own class now	0	1	2	3	4	5
I think that Sunflowers has had a positive effect on the whole school	0	1	2	3	4	5

Any other comments about Sunflowers

Positive Intervention for Pupils who Struggle at School, Routledge © Helen Sonnet 2010

Greeting	Counting	Circle activities
Cooking	Art	Science
PSHE	Drama	Group game
Board games	Wash up/story time	Clapping rhyme/song/goodbye

Positive Intervention for Pupils who Struggle at School, Routledge © Helen Sonnet 2010

Designs for place mats

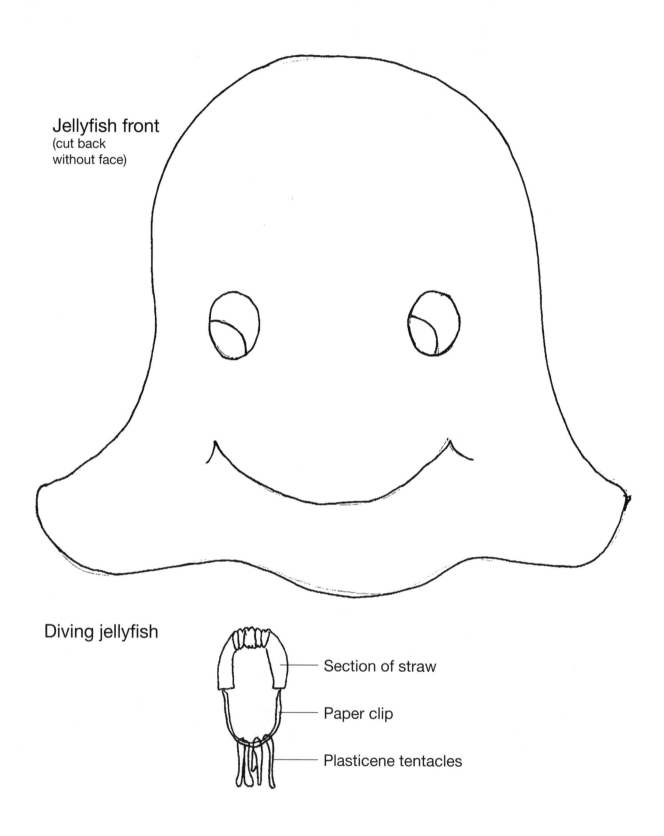

Jellyfish front
(cut back
without face)

Diving jellyfish

— Section of straw

— Paper clip

— Plasticene tentacles

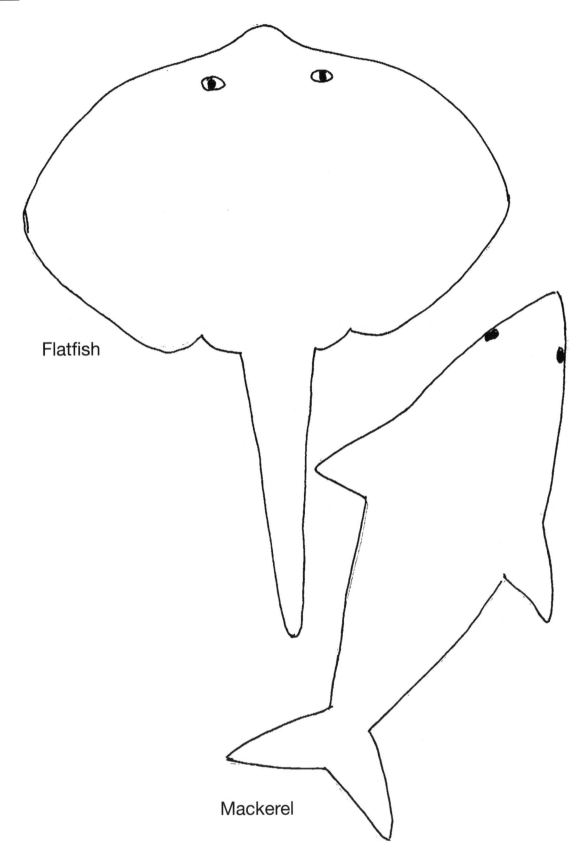

Flatfish

Mackerel

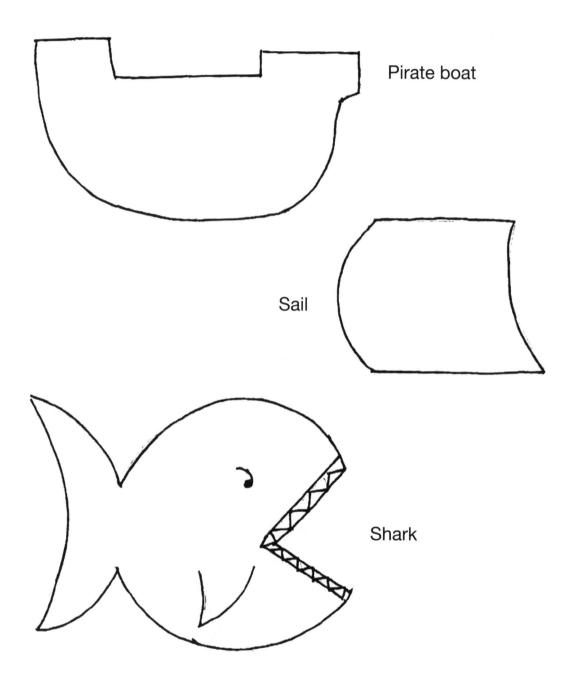

Pirate boat

Sail

Shark

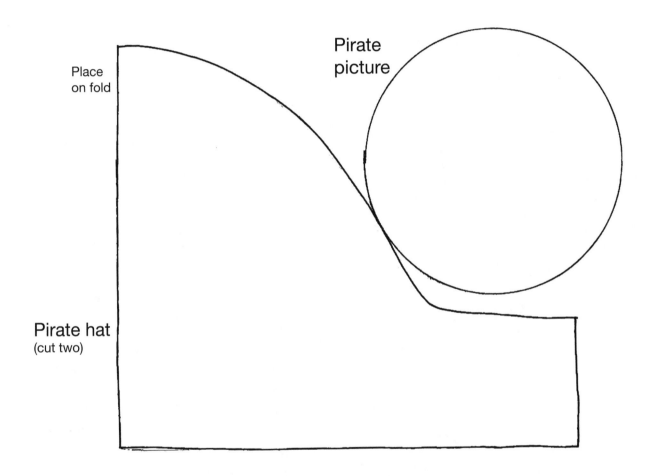

Pirate
picture

Place
on fold

Pirate hat
(cut two)

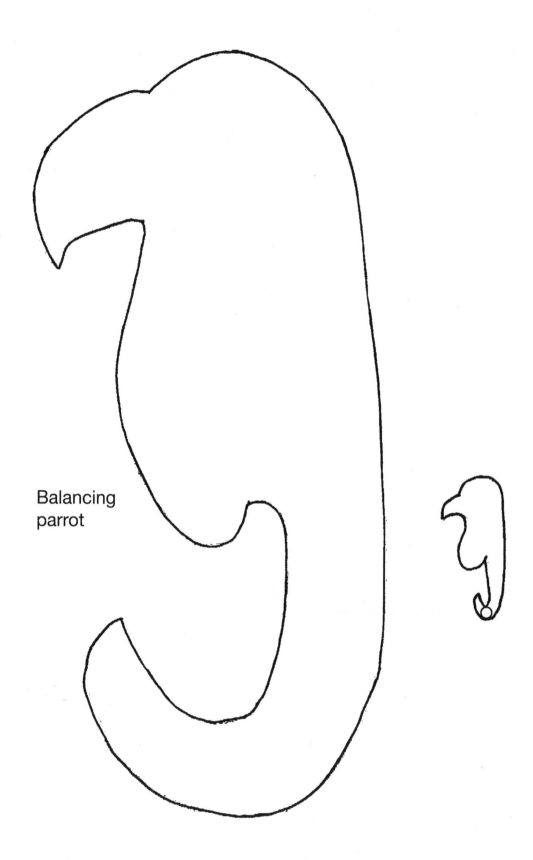

Balancing
parrot